CORPORATE FINANCE WORKBOOK

CFA Institute is the premier association for investment professionals around the world, with over 101,000 members in 134 countries. Since 1963 the organization has developed and administered the renowned Chartered Financial Analyst® Program. With a rich history of leading the investment profession, CFA Institute has set the highest standards in ethics, education, and professional excellence within the global investment community, and is the foremost authority on investment profession conduct and practice.

Each book in the CFA Institute Investment Series is geared toward industry practitioners along with graduate-level finance students and covers the most important topics in the industry. The authors of these cutting-edge books are themselves industry professionals and academics and bring their wealth of knowledge and expertise to this series.

CORPORATE FINANCE WORKBOOK

A Practical Approach

Second Edition

Michelle R. Clayman, CFA

Martin S. Fridson, CFA

George H. Troughton, CFA

WILEY

John Wiley & Sons, Inc.

For general information on our other products and services or for technical support, please contact our Customer Care Department within the United States at (800) 762-2974, outside the United States at (317) 572-3993 or fax (317) 572-4002.

Wiley also publishes its books in a variety of electronic formats. Some content that appears in print may not be available in electronic books. For more information about Wiley products, visit our web site at www.wiley.com.

ISBN 978-1-118-11197-0 (paper); ISBN 978-1-118-21726-9 (ebk);
ISBN 978-1-118-21727-6 (ebk); ISBN 978-1-118-21728-3 (ebk)

Printed in the United States of America

10 9 8 7 6 5 4 3 2 1

CONTENTS

PART I

LEARNING OUTCOMES, SUMMARY OVERVIEW, AND PROBLEMS

CHAPTER 1

CORPORATE GOVERNANCE

LEARNING OUTCOMES

After completing this chapter, you will be able to do the following:

- Explain corporate governance, describe the objectives and core attributes of an effective corporate governance system, and evaluate whether a company's corporate governance has those attributes.
- Compare major business forms and describe the conflicts of interest associated with each.
- Explain conflicts that arise in agency relationships, including manager-shareholder conflicts and director-shareholder conflicts.
- Describe responsibilities of the board of directors and explain qualifications and core competencies that an investment analyst should look for in the board of directors.
- Explain effective corporate governance practice as it relates to the board of directors, and evaluate the strengths and weaknesses of a company's corporate governance practice.
- Describe elements of a company's statement of corporate governance policies that investment analysts should assess.
- Explain the valuation implications of corporate governance.

SUMMARY OVERVIEW

- Corporate governance is the system of principles, policies, procedures, and clearly defined responsibilities and accountabilities, used by stakeholders to eliminate or minimize conflicts of interest.
- The objectives of a corporate governance system are (1) to eliminate or mitigate conflicts of interest among stakeholders, particularly between managers and shareholders, and (2) to ensure that the assets of the company are used efficiently and productively and in the best interests of the investors and other stakeholders.
- The failure of a company to establish an effective system of corporate governance represents a major operational risk to the company and its investors. To understand the risks inherent in an investment in a company, it is essential to understand the quality of the company's corporate governance practices.
- The core attributes of an effective corporate governance system are:
  a. Delineation of the rights of shareholders and other core stakeholders
  b. Clearly defined manager and director governance responsibilities to the stakeholders

    c. Identifiable and measurable accountabilities for the performance of the responsibilities
    d. Fairness and equitable treatment in all dealings between managers, directors, and shareholders
    e. Complete transparency and accuracy in disclosures regarding operations, performance, risk, and financial position
- The specific sources of conflict in corporate agency relationships are
    a. Manager-shareholder conflicts—Managers may, for example:
      - Use funds to try to expand the size of a business even when this is not in the best interests of shareholders
      - Grant themselves numerous expensive perquisites that are treated as ordinary business expenses
    b. Director-Shareholder Conflicts—Directors may, for example, identify with the managers' interests rather than those of the shareholders as a result of personal or business relationships with the manager.
- The responsibilities of board members, both individually and as a group, are to
    a. Establish corporate values and governance structures for the company to ensure that the business is conducted in an ethical, competent, fair, and professional manner
    b. Ensure that all legal and regulatory requirements are met and complied with fully and in a timely fashion
    c. Establish long-term strategic objectives for the company with a goal of ensuring that the best interests of shareholders come first and that the company's obligations to others are met in a timely and complete manner
    d. Establish clear lines of responsibility and a strong system of accountability and performance measurement in all phases of a company's operations
    e. Hire the chief executive officer, determine the compensation package, and periodically evaluate the officer's performance
    f. Ensure that management has supplied the board with sufficient information for it to be fully informed and prepared to make the decisions that are its responsibility, and to be able to adequately monitor and oversee the company's management
    g. Meet regularly to perform its duties and in extraordinary session as required by events
    h. Acquire adequate training so that members are able to adequately perform their duties
- An investor or investment analyst must assess
    a. Board composition and independence
    b. Whether the chairman of the board is independent
    c. The qualifications of the directors
    d. Whether the board is elected on an annual or staggered basis
    e. Board self-assessment practices
    f. The frequency of separate sessions of independent directors
    g. The audit committee and audit oversight
    h. The nominating committee
    i. The compensation committee and compensation awards to management
    j. The use (or not) of independent legal and expert counsel
- Companies committed to corporate governance often provide a statement of corporate governance policies. Analysts should assess: the code of ethics; statements of the oversight, monitoring, and review responsibilities of directors; statements of management's responsibilities with respect to information and access of directors to internal company functions; reports of directors' examinations, evaluations, and findings; board and committee self-assessments; management self-assessments; and training policies for directors.

- Weak corporate governance systems give rise to risks including accounting risk, asset risk, liability risk, and strategic policy risk. Such risks may compromise the value of investments in the company.

PROBLEMS

1. Which of the following *best* defines the concept of corporate governance?
   A. A system for monitoring managers' activities, rewarding performance, and disciplining misbehavior.
   B. Corporate values and governance structures that ensure the business is conducted in an ethical, competent, fair, and professional manner.
   C. A system of principles, policies, and procedures used to manage and control the activities of a corporation so as to overcome conflicts of interest inherent in the corporate form.

2. Which of the following is an example of a conflict of interest that an effective corporate governance system would mitigate or eliminate?
   A. A majority of the board is independent of management.
   B. Directors identify with the managers' interests rather than those of the shareholders.
   C. Directors have board experience with companies regarded as having sound governance practices.

3. Which of the following *best* describes the corporate governance responsibilities of members of the board of directors?
   A. Establish long-term strategic objectives for the company.
   B. Ensure that at board meetings no subject is undiscussable and dissent is regarded as an obligation.
   C. Ensure that the board negotiates with the company over all matters such as compensation.

4. Which of the following is *least likely* to be useful in evaluating a company's corporate governance system for investment analysis purposes?
   A. Assess issues related to the board, managers, and shareholders.
   B. Review the company's regulatory filings and financial information provided to shareholders.
   C. Flag items such as egregious use of insider transactions for users of the financial statements.

5. The objectives of an effective system of corporate governance include all of the following *except*:
   A. ensure that the assets of the company are used efficiently and productively.
   B. eliminate or mitigate conflicts of interest among stakeholders.
   C. ensure complete transparency in disclosures regarding operations, performance, risk, and financial position.

6. All of the following are core attributes of an effective corporate governance system *except*:
   A. fairness and accuracy in identifying inherent conflicts of interest.
   B. clearly defined governance responsibilities for managers and directors.
   C. delineation of shareholders and other core stakeholders' rights.

7. All of the following are examples of conflicts of interest that an effective corporate governance system should address *except* relationships between:
    A. managers and shareholders.
    B. managers and directors.
    C. managers and institutional analysts.

8. All of the following are true of an effective system of corporate governance *except*:
    A. the system must be continually monitored especially with changes in management and the board.
    B. a single system of effective corporate governance applies to all firms worldwide.
    C. there are a number of common characteristics of all sound corporate governance structures.

The following information relates to Questions 9–14.

Jane Smith, CFA, has recently joined Zero Asset Management, Inc. (Zero) as a board member. Since Smith is also outside council for Zero, she is already very familiar with Zero's operations and expects to begin contributing good ideas right away. Zero is a publicly traded investment management firm that historically focused on mutual fund management. Although there is current market opportunity to add a new type of mutual fund, the board recently decided against adding the fund. Instead, the board decided to expand its business to include a hedge fund operation within the existing corporation.

Bill Week, CEO of Zero, has publicly stated that he is willing to bet the company's future on hedge fund management. Week is the founder of Zero, as well as Chairman of the board, and maintains a controlling interest in the company.

Like the rest of Zero, the firm's new hedge fund is quantitatively driven and index based. The fund has been set up in a separate office with new systems so that the analysts and managers can create a unique hedge-fund culture. Trading and execution are the only operations that remain with Zero. The fund is run by one of Zero's most successful portfolio managers.

Smith learns that although none of the board members sit on other companies' boards, most have at one point or another worked at Zero and so they are very familiar with Zero's operations. A board member has attempted to make the health insurance and retirement concerns of the board members an agenda item, without success to date. Smith eagerly anticipates the next board meeting as they are always in a luxurious setting.

At the board meeting, Smith asks a number of questions about Zero's corporate governance system. The board becomes concerned by Smith's questions and decides to hire an independent consultant to review their corporate governance responsibilities. The consultant starts his analysis by stating that a corporate governance system relies upon checks and balances among managers, directors, and investors. Smith asks if Zero has the proper systems in place. The consultant says that he has looked at conflicts of interest and has one more area to review in order to verify that the board is meeting its major objectives. Concerned about the company's stock price, Smith asks the consultant what work he has done concerning Zero's corporate disclosures for investment professionals. The consultant indicates that he has reviewed Zero's regulatory filings for clear and complete information, as well as the company's policies regarding related party transactions.

9. All of the following indicate Zero's board's lack of independence *except*:
    A. personal relationships.
    B. service of the outside counsel as a board member.
    C. lack of interlocking directorships.

10. Which of the following is the most effective action for the board to take to address their oversight responsibilities concerning the hedge fund's proxy voting?
    A. Establish corporate values and governance structure for the company.
    B. Establish long-term strategic objectives that are met and fully complied with.
    C. Perform adequate training so that employees are able to perform their duties.

11. Which of the following omissions best describes a corporate governance shortcoming of Zero's board of directors? The board's failure to:
    A. address the potential conflicts of interest between managing the firm's hedge fund and its mutual fund business.
    B. meet the market opportunity for a new kind of mutual fund.
    C. establish the hedge fund operation in a separate corporation.

12. Given that Zero's directors all previously worked at the company, which of the following would you recommend for a more effective system of corporate governance?
    A. Ensure that assets are used efficiently and productively and in the best interests of investors and stakeholders.
    B. Eliminate or mitigate conflicts of interest among stakeholders, particularly between managers and shareholders.
    C. Identify and measure accountabilities for the performance of the board's responsibilities.

13. Which of the following best describes the objectives of Zero's board that the consultant has not yet reviewed? The board should ensure:
    A. that the assets of the company are used efficiently and productively and in the best interests of the investors and other stakeholders.
    B. that material foreseeable risk factors are addressed and considered.
    C. compliance with applicable laws and take into account the interest of stakeholders.

14. Which of the following is the most critical activity that an analyst can engage in to assess the quality of the corporate governance system at Zero, among those that the consultant did not review?
    A. Look for vague references to off-balance-sheet or insider information.
    B. Identify the responsiveness of the board to shareholder proxy votes.
    C. Evaluate the quality and extent of financial information provided to investors.

The following information relates to Questions 15–19.

Shelley Newcome is the new CEO for a publicly traded financial services company, Asset Management Co. (AMC). Newcome is new to the corporate governance requirements of a publicly traded company, as she previously worked for a family office that invested in private equity.

At her first board meeting, the company's first in six months, she asks a director what the objectives of corporate governance should be. The director tells her that the most important objective he can think of is to eliminate or mitigate conflicts of interest among stakeholders.

One of Newcome's first steps as CEO is to fly to New York City in order to address a group of Wall Street analysts. Newcome is happy to discover that AMC provides her, and other senior management, with a company jet to attend such meetings.

At the opening of the meeting, Newcome is surprised to hear that most of the analysts are extremely interested in learning about AMC's corporate governance system. One analyst indicates that he has studied several of AMC's competitors and found that they share a set of critical and core attributes. The analyst goes on to note that like its competitors, AMC has included in its corporate governance system the following attributes: the rights of shareholders and other core stakeholders are clearly delineated; there is complete transparency and accuracy in disclosures regarding operations, performance, risk, and financial position; and identifiable and measurable accountabilities for the performance of responsibilities. The analyst also says that in order to verify that the board is meeting its major objectives he has looked at AMC's conflicts of interest and has one more area to review.

Newcome then asks the analyst why his corporate governance evaluation of AMC is so important. The analyst responds by saying that his decision whether or not to invest in AMC, and ultimately the long-term performance of the company, is dependent upon the quality of AMC's managers' decisions and the skill they use in applying sound management practices.

Closing the meeting, Newcome is delayed by one analyst who complains about the difficulties of flying these days and how he has to get to the airport hours ahead of time. The analyst goes on to say that he reviewed AMC's regulatory filings and was happy to see that the company does not spend its money on frivolous perquisites like executive jets.

15. Which of the following would *best* complete the objectives of corporate governance for the CEO?
    A. Ensure that assets of the company are used efficiently and productively and in the best interests of investors and other stakeholders.
    B. Clearly define governance responsibilities for both managers and directors.
    C. Establish clear lines of responsibility and a strong system of accountability and performance measurement in all phases of a company's operations.

16. On the basis of the Wall Street analyst comments about AMC's corporate governance system, which of the following would be *most* effective for AMC to attract investors' interest?
    A. Implement a corporate governance system in which business activity is encouraged and rewarded, and that leads to innovation.
    B. Establish a corporate governance system that overcomes inherent conflicts of interest since they represent a major operational risk to investors and the continued existence of the company.
    C. Provide full transparency of all material information on a timely basis to all investment analysts.

17. Which of the following is a core attribute that the Wall Street analyst left out of his analysis of AMC?
    A. Corporate governance systems rely on checks and balances among managers, directors, and investors.
    B. Fairness in all dealings between managers, directors, and shareholders.
    C. Complete, accurate, and transparent disclosure of loans to private equity funds.

18. Based on the information provided in the case, which of the following corporate disclosures could investment professionals use to evaluate the quality of the corporate governance system at AMC?
    A. Inclusion of all vague references to off-balance sheet or insider transactions in board minutes.
    B. Failure to disclose executive perquisites such as the use of corporate jets by senior management.
    C. Provide other compensation that has not been disclosed to investment analysts.

19. Which of the following is an example of a corporate governance responsibility that AMC's board of directors has failed to meet?
    A. Ensure that the board adequately monitors and oversees the company's management.
    B. Ensure that management has supplied the board with sufficient information for it to be fully informed.
    C. Meet regularly to perform its duties.

CHAPTER 2

CAPITAL BUDGETING

LEARNING OUTCOMES

After completing this chapter, you will be able to do the following:

- Describe the capital budgeting process, including the typical steps of the process, and distinguish among the various categories of capital projects.
- Describe the basic principles of capital budgeting, including cash flow estimation.
- Explain how the evaluation and selection of capital projects is affected by mutually exclusive projects, project sequencing, and capital rationing.
- Calculate and interpret the results using each of the following methods to evaluate a single capital project: net present value (NPV), internal rate of return (IRR), payback period, discounted payback period, average accounting rate of return (AAR), and profitability index (PI).
- Explain the NPV profile, compare NPV and IRR methods when evaluating independent and mutually exclusive projects, and describe the problems associated with each of the evaluation methods.
- Describe the relative popularity of the various capital budgeting methods and explain the relation between NPV and company value and stock price.
- Describe the expected relations among an investment's NPV, company value, and stock price.
- Calculate the yearly cash flows of an expansion capital project and a replacement capital project, and evaluate how the choice of depreciation method affects those cash flows.
- Explain the effects of inflation on capital budgeting analysis.
- Evaluate and select the optimal capital project in situations of (1) mutually exclusive projects with unequal lives, using either the least common multiple of lives approach or the equivalent annual annuity approach, and (2) capital rationing.
- Explain how sensitivity analysis, scenario analysis, and Monte Carlo simulation can be used to estimate the standalone risk of a capital project.
- Explain the procedure for determining the discount rate to be used in valuing a capital project and calculate a project's required rate of return using the capital asset pricing model (CAPM).
- Describe the types of real options and evaluate the profitability of investments with real options.
- Explain capital budgeting pitfalls.
- Calculate and interpret accounting income and economic income in the context of capital budgeting.
- Distinguish among and evaluate a capital project using the economic profit, residual income, and claims valuation models.

SUMMARY OVERVIEW

- Capital budgeting undergirds the most critical investments for many corporations—their investments in long-term assets. The principles of capital budgeting have been applied to other corporate investing and financing decisions and to security analysis and portfolio management.
- The typical steps in the capital budgeting process are: (1) generating ideas, (2) analyzing individual proposals, (3) planning the capital budget, and (4) monitoring and post-auditing.
- Projects susceptible to capital budgeting process can be categorized as: (1) replacement, (2) expansion, (3) new products and services, and (4) regulatory, safety, and environmental.
- Capital budgeting decisions are based on incremental after-tax cash flows discounted at the opportunity cost of funds. Financing costs are ignored because both the cost of debt and the cost of other capital are captured in the discount rate.
- The net present value (NPV) is the present value of all after-tax cash flows, or

$$NPV = \sum_{t=0}^{n} \frac{CF_t}{(1+r)^t}$$

where the investment outlays are negative cash flows included in the $CF_t s$ and where r is the required rate of return for the investment.
- The IRR is the discount rate that makes the present value of all future cash flows sum to zero. This equation can be solved for the IRR:

$$\sum_{t=0}^{n} \frac{CF_t}{(1+IRR)^t} = 0$$

- The payback period is the number of years required to recover the original investment in a project. The payback is based on cash flows.
- The discounted payback period is the number of years it takes for the cumulative discounted cash flows from a project to equal the original investment.
- The average accounting rate of return (AAR) can be defined as follows:

$$AAR = \frac{Average\ net\ income}{Average\ book\ value}$$

- The profitability index (PI) is the present value of a project's future cash flows divided by the initial investment:

$$PI = \frac{PV\ of\ future\ cash\ flows}{Initial\ investment} = 1 + \frac{NPV}{Initial\ investment}$$

- The capital budgeting decision rules are to invest if the NPV > 0, if the IRR > r, or if the PI > 1.0. There are no decision rules for the payback period, discounted payback period, and AAR because they are not always sound measures.
- The NPV profile is a graph that shows a project's NPV graphed as a function of various discount rates.
- For mutually exclusive projects that are ranked differently by the NPV and IRR, it is economically sound to choose the project with the higher NPV.

- The "multiple IRR problem" and the "no IRR problem" can arise for a project with nonconventional cash flows—cash flows that change signs more than once during the project's life.
- The fact that projects with positive NPVs theoretically increase the value of the company and the value of its stock could explain the popularity of NPV as an evaluation method.
- Analysts often organize the cash flows for capital budgeting in tables, summing all of the cash flows occurring at each point in time. These totals are then used to find an NPV or IRR. Alternatively, tables collecting cash flows by type can be used. Equations for the capital budgeting cash flows are as follows:

  Initial outlay:

  $$\text{Outlay} = \text{FCInv} + \text{NWCInv} - \text{Sal}_0 + T(\text{Sal}_0 - B_0)$$

  Annual after-tax operating cash flow:

  $$\text{CF} = (S - C - D)(1 - T) + D, \text{ or}$$

  $$\text{CF} = (S - C)(1 - D) + TD$$

  Terminal year after-tax nonoperating cash flow:

  $$\text{TNOCF} = \text{Sal}_T + \text{NWCInv} - T(\text{Sal}_T - B_T)$$

- Depreciation schedules affect taxable income, taxes paid, and after-tax cash flows, and therefore capital budgeting valuations.
- Spreadsheets are heavily used for capital budgeting valuation.
- When inflation exists, the analyst should perform capital budgeting analysis in "nominal" terms if cash flows are nominal and in "real" terms if cash flows are real.
- Inflation reduces the value of depreciation tax savings (unless the tax system adjusts depreciation for inflation). Inflation reduces the value of fixed payments to bondholders. Inflation usually does not affect all revenues and costs uniformly. Contracting with customers, suppliers, employees, and sources of capital can be complicated as inflation rises.
- Two ways of comparing mutually exclusive projects in a replacement chain are the "least common multiple of lives" approach and the "equivalent annual annuity" approach.
- For the least common multiple of lives approach, the analyst extends the time horizon of analysis so that the lives of both projects will divide exactly into the horizon. The projects are replicated over this horizon, and the NPV for the total cash flows over the least common multiple of lives is used to evaluate the investments.
- The equivalent annual annuity is the annuity payment (series of equal annual payments over the project's life) that is equivalent in value to the project's actual cash flows. Analysts find the present value of all of the cash flows for an investment (the NPV) and then calculate an annuity payment that has a value equivalent to the NPV.
- With capital rationing, the company's capital budget has a size constraint. Under "hard" capital rationing, the budget is fixed. In the case of hard rationing, managers use trial and error and sometimes mathematical programming to find the optimal set of projects. In that situation, it is best to use the NPV or PI valuation methods.
- Sensitivity analysis calculates the effect on the NPV of changes in one input variable at a time.
- Scenario analysis creates scenarios that consist of changes in several of the input variables and calculates the NPV for each scenario.

- Simulation (Monte Carlo) analysis is used to estimate probability distributions for the NPV or IRR of a capital project. Simulations randomly select values for stochastic input variables and then repeatedly calculate the project NPV and IRR to find their distributions.
- Risk-adjusted discount rates based on market risk measures should be used as the required rate of return for projects when the investors are diversified. The capital asset pricing model (CAPM) and arbitrage pricing theory (APT) are common approaches for finding market-based risk-adjusted rates.
- In the CAPM, a project's or asset's beta, or β, is used as a measure of systematic risk. The security market line (SML) estimates the asset's required rate of return as $r_i = R_F + \beta_i[E(R_M) - R_F]$.
- Project-specific betas should be used instead of company betas whenever the risk of the project differs from that of the company.
- Real options can be classified as (1) timing options; (2) sizing options, which can be abandonment options or growth (expansion) options; (3) flexibility options, which can be price-setting options or production-flexibility options; and (4) fundamental options. Simple options can be evaluated with decision trees; for more complex options, the analyst should use option pricing models.
- Economic income is the investment's after-tax cash flow plus the change in the market value. Accounting income is revenues minus expenses. Accounting depreciation, based on the original cost of the investment, is the decrease in the book (accounting) value, while economic depreciation is the decrease in the market value of the investment. Accounting net income is net of the after-tax interest expenses on the company's debt obligations. In computing economic income, financing costs are ignored.
- Economic profit is

$$EP = NOPAT - \$WACC$$

where $NOPAT = $ Net operating profit after tax $= EBIT(1 - Tax\ rate)$ and $\$WACC = $ Dollar cost of capital $= WACC \times Capital$. When applied to the valuation of an asset or security, the NPV of an investment (and its market value added) is the present value of future EP discounted at the weighted average cost of capital.

$$NPV = MVA = \sum_{t=1}^{\infty} \frac{EP_t}{(1 + WACC)^t}$$

The total value of the company (of the asset) is the original investment plus the NPV.

- Residual income $=$ Net income $-$ Equity charge, or $RI_t = NI_t - r_e B_{t-1}$ where $RI_t = $ Residual income during period t, $NI_t = $ Net income during period t, $r_e = $ the cost of equity, and $B_{t-1} = $ the beginning-of-period book value of equity. The NPV of an investment is the present value of future residual income discounted at the required rate of return on equity:

$$NPV = \sum_{t=1}^{\infty} \frac{RI_t}{(1 + r_e)^t}$$

- The total value of the company (of the asset) is the NPV plus the original equity investment plus the original debt investment.
- The claims valuation approach values an asset by valuing the claims against the asset. For example, an asset financed with debt and equity has a value equal to the value of the debt plus the value of the equity.

PROBLEMS

1. Given the following cash flows for a capital project, calculate the NPV and IRR. The required rate of return is 8%.

Year	0	1	2	3	4	5
Cash flow	−50,000	15,000	15,000	20,000	10,000	5,000

     NPV   IRR
A. $1,905 10.9%
B. $1,905 26.0%
C. $3,379 10.9%

2. Given the following cash flows for a capital project, calculate its payback period and discounted payback period. The required rate of return is 8%. The discounted payback period is:

Year	0	1	2	3	4	5
Cash flow	−50,000	15,000	15,000	20,000	10,000	5,000

A. 0.16 years longer than the payback period.
B. 0.51 years longer than the payback period.
C. 1.01 years longer than the payback period.

3. An investment of $100 generates after-tax cash flows of $40 in Year 1, $80 in Year 2, and $120 in Year 3. The required rate of return is 20%. The net present value is *closest* to:
A. $42.22.
B. $58.33.
C. $68.52.

4. An investment of $150,000 is expected to generate an after-tax cash flow of $100,000 in one year and another $120,000 in two years. The cost of capital is 10%. What is the internal rate of return?
A. 28.39%.
B. 28.59%.
C. 28.79%.

5. Kim Corporation is considering an investment of 750 million won with expected after-tax cash inflows of 175 million won per year for seven years. The required rate of return is 10%. What is the project's

	NPV?	IRR?
A.	102 million won	14.0%
B.	157 million won	23.3%
C.	193 million won	10.0%

6. Kim Corporation is considering an investment of 750 million won with expected after-tax cash inflows of 175 million won per year for seven years. The required rate of return is 10%. Expressed in years, the project's payback period and discounted payback period, respectively, are *closest* to:
   A. 4.3 years and 5.4 years.
   B. 4.3 years and 5.9 years.
   C. 4.8 years and 6.3 years.

7. An investment of $20,000 will create a perpetual after-tax cash flow of $2,000. The required rate of return is 8%. What is the investment's profitability index?
   A. 1.08.
   B. 1.16.
   C. 1.25.

8. Hermann Corporation is considering an investment of €375 million with expected after-tax cash inflows of €115 million per year for seven years and an additional after-tax salvage value of €50 million in year seven. The required rate of return is 10%. What is the investment's PI?
   A. 1.19.
   B. 1.33.
   C. 1.56.

9. Erin Chou is reviewing a profitable investment project that has a conventional cash flow pattern. If the cash flows for the project, initial outlay, and future after-tax cash flows all double, Chou would predict that the IRR would:
   A. increase and the NPV would increase.
   B. stay the same and the NPV would increase.
   C. stay the same and the NPV would stay the same.

10. Shirley Shea has evaluated an investment proposal and found that its payback period is one year, it has a negative NPV, and it has a positive IRR. Is this combination of results possible?
    A. Yes.
    B. No, because a project with a positive IRR has a positive NPV.
    C. No, because a project with such a rapid payback period has a positive NPV.

11. An investment has an outlay of 100 and after-tax cash flows of 40 annually for four years. A project enhancement increases the outlay by 15 and the annual after-tax cash flows by 5. As a result, the vertical intercept of the NPV profile of the enhanced project shifts:
    A. up and the horizontal intercept shifts left.
    B. up and the horizontal intercept shifts right.
    C. down and the horizontal intercept shifts left.

12. Projects 1 and 2 have similar outlays, although the patterns of future cash flows are different. The cash flows as well as the NPV and IRR for the two projects are shown in the following table. For both projects, the required rate of return is 10%.

| | Cash Flows | | | | | | |
Year	0	1	2	3	4	NPV	IRR
Project 1	−50	20	20	20	20	13.40	21.86%
Project 2	−50	0	0	0	100	18.30	18.92%

The two projects are mutually exclusive. What is the appropriate investment decision?
A. Invest in both projects.
B. Invest in Project 1 because it has the higher IRR.
C. Invest in Project 2 because it has the higher NPV.

13. Consider the two projects below. The cash flows as well as the NPV and IRR for the two projects are given. For both projects, the required rate of return is 10%.

| | Cash Flows | | | | | | |
Year	0	1	2	3	4	NPV	IRR
Project 1	−100	36	36	36	36	14.12	16.37%
Project 2	−100	0	0	0	175	19.53	15.02%

What discount rate would result in the same NPV for both projects?
A. A rate between 0.00% and 10.00%.
B. A rate between 10.00% and 15.02%.
C. A rate between 15.02% and 16.37%.

14. Wilson Flannery is concerned that this project has multiple IRRs.

Year	0	1	2	3
Cash flows	−50	100	0	−50

How many discount rates produce a zero NPV for this project?
A. One, a discount rate of 0%.
B. Two, discount rates of 0% and 32%.
C. Two, discount rates of 0% and 62%.

15. With regard to the net present value (NPV) profiles of two projects, the crossover rate is *best* described as the discount rate at which:
A. two projects have the same NPV.
B. two projects have the same internal rate of return.
C. a project's NPV changes from positive to negative.

16. With regard to net present value (NPV) profiles, the point at which a profile crosses the vertical axis is *best* described as:
A. the point at which two projects have the same NPV.
B. the sum of the undiscounted cash flows from a project.
C. a project's internal rate of return when the project's NPV is equal to zero.

17. With regard to net present value (NPV) profiles, the point at which a profile crosses the horizontal axis is *best* described as:
   A. the point at which two projects have the same NPV.
   B. the sum of the undiscounted cash flows from a project.
   C. a project's internal rate of return when the project's NPV is equal to zero.

18. With regard to capital budgeting, an appropriate estimate of the incremental cash flows from a project is *least likely* to include:
   A. externalities.
   B. interest costs.
   C. opportunity costs.

19. FITCO is considering the purchase of new equipment. The equipment costs $350,000, and an additional $110,000 is needed to install it. The equipment will be depreciated straight-line to zero over a five-year life. The equipment will generate additional annual revenues of $265,000, and it will have annual cash operating expenses of $83,000. The equipment will be sold for $85,000 after five years. An inventory investment of $73,000 is required during the life of the investment. FITCO is in the 40% tax bracket and its cost of capital is 10%. What is the project NPV?
   A. $52,122.
   B. $64,090.
   C. $97,449.

20. After estimating a project's NPV, the analyst is advised that the fixed capital outlay will be revised upward by $100,000. The fixed capital outlay is depreciated straight-line over an eight-year life. The tax rate is 40% and the required rate of return is 10%. No changes in cash operating revenues, cash operating expenses, or salvage value are expected. What is the effect on the project NPV?
   A. $100,000 decrease.
   B. $73,325 decrease.
   C. $59,988 decrease.

21. When assembling the cash flows to calculate an NPV or IRR, the project's after-tax interest expenses should be subtracted from the cash flows for:
   A. the IRR calculation, but not the NPV calculation.
   B. both the NPV calculation and the IRR calculation.
   C. neither the NPV calculation nor the IRR calculation.

22. Standard Corporation is investing $400,000 of fixed capital in a project that will be depreciated straight-line to zero over its 10-year life. Annual sales are expected to be $240,000, and annual cash operating expenses are expected to be $110,000. An investment of $40,000 in net working capital is required over the project's life. The corporate income tax rate is 30 percent. What is the after-tax operating cash flow expected in year one?
   A. $63,000.
   B. $92,000.
   C. $103,000.

23. Five years ago, Frater Zahn's Company invested £38 million—£30 million in fixed capital and another £8 million in working capital—in a bakery. Today, Frater Zahn's

is selling the fixed assets for £21 million and liquidating the investment in working capital. The book value of the fixed assets is £15 million and the marginal tax rate is 40%. The fifth year's after-tax nonoperating cash flow to Frater Zahn's is *closest* to:
A. £20.6 million.
B. £23.0 million.
C. £26.6 million.

The following information relates to Questions 24, 25, and 26.

McConachie Company is considering the purchase of a new 400-ton stamping press. The press costs $360,000, and an additional $40,000 is needed to install it. The press will be depreciated straight-line to zero over a five-year life. The press will generate no additional revenues, but it will reduce cash operating expenses by $140,000 annually. The press will be sold for $120,000 after five years. An inventory investment of $60,000 is required during the life of the investment. McConachie is in the 40 percent tax bracket.

24. What is the McConachie net investment outlay?
    A. $400,000.
    B. $420,000.
    C. $460,000.

25. McConachie's incremental annual after-tax operating cash flow is *closest* to:
    A. $116,000.
    B. $124,000.
    C. $140,000.

26. What is the terminal year after-tax nonoperating cash flow at the end of year five?
    A. $108,000.
    B. $132,000.
    C. $180,000.

The following information relates to Questions 27 through 32.

Linda Pyle is head of analyst recruiting for PPA Securities. She has been very frustrated by the number of job applicants who, in spite of their stellar pedigrees, seem to have little understanding of basic financial concepts. Pyle has written a set of conceptual questions and simple problems for the human resources department to use to screen for the better candidates in the applicant pool. A few of her corporate finance questions and problems are given below.

Concept 1.   "A company invests in depreciable assets, financed partly by issuing fixed-rate bonds. If inflation is lower than expected, the value of the real tax savings from depreciation and the value of the real after-tax interest expense are both reduced."

Concept 2.   "Sensitivity analysis and scenario analysis are useful tools for estimating the impact on a project's NPV of changing the value of one capital budgeting input variable at a time."

Concept 3.   "When comparing two mutually exclusive projects with unequal lives, the IRR is a good approach for choosing the better project because it does not require equal lives."

Concept 4.   "Project-specific betas should be used instead of company betas whenever the risk of the project differs from that of the company."

Problem.   "Fontenot Company is investing €100 in a project that is being depreciated straight-line to zero over a two-year life with no salvage value. The project will generate earnings before interest and taxes of €50 each year for two years. Fontenot's weighted average cost of capital and required rate of return for the project are both 12 percent, and its tax rate is 30 percent."

27. For Concept 1, the statement is correct regarding the effects on:
    A. the real tax savings from depreciation, but incorrect regarding the real after-tax interest expense.
    B. both the real tax savings from depreciation and the real after-tax interest expense.
    C. neither the real tax savings from depreciation nor the real after-tax interest expense.

28. For Concept 2, the statement is correct regarding:
    A. sensitivity analysis, but not correct regarding scenario analysis.
    B. scenario analysis, but not correct regarding sensitivity analysis.
    C. both sensitivity analysis and scenario analysis.

29. Are the statements identified as Concept 3 and Concept 4 correct?
    A. No for Concepts 3 and 4.
    B. No for Concept 3, but yes for Concept 4.
    C. Yes for Concept 3, but no for Concept 4.

30. The after-tax operating cash flows in euros for the Fontenot Company are:
    A. 50 in both years.
    B. 70 in both years.
    C. 85 in both years.

31. The economic income in euros for the Fontenot Company is:
    A. 17.24 in year one and 9.11 in year two.
    B. 17.76 in year one and 24.89 in year two.
    C. 24.89 in year one and 17.76 in year two.

32. The market value added (MVA) in euros for the Fontenot Company is *closest* to:
    A. 38.87.
    B. 39.92.
    C. 43.65.

The following information relates to Questions 33–38.

The capital budgeting committee for Laroche Industries is meeting. Laroche is a North American conglomerate that has several divisions. One of these divisions, Laroche Livery, operates a large fleet of vans. Laroche's management is evaluating whether it is optimal to operate new vans for two, three, or four years before replacing them. The managers have estimated the investment outlay, annual after-tax operating expenses, and after-tax salvage cash flows for each of the service lives. Because revenues and some operating costs are unaffected by the choice of service life, they were ignored in the analysis. Laroche Livery's opportunity cost of funds is 10 percent. The following table gives the cash flows in thousands of Canadian dollars (C$).

Service Life	Investment	Year 1	Year 2	Year 3	Year 4	Salvage
2 years	−40,000	−12,000	−15,000			20,000
3 years	−40,000	−12,000	−15,000	−20,000		17,000
4 years	−40,000	−12,000	−15,000	−20,000	−25,000	12,000

Schoeman Products, another division of Laroche, has evaluated several investment projects and now must choose the subset of them that fits within its C$40 million capital budget. The outlays and NPVs for the six projects are given below. Schoeman cannot buy fractional projects, and must buy all or none of a project. The currency amounts are in millions of Canadian dollars.

Project	Outlay	PV of Future Cash Flows	NPV
1	31	44	13
2	15	21	6
3	12	16.5	4.5
4	10	13	3
5	8	11	3
6	6	8	2

Schoeman wants to determine which subset of the six projects is optimal.

A final proposal comes from the division Society Services, which has an investment opportunity with a real option to invest further if conditions warrant. The crucial details are as follows:

- The original project:
  - An outlay of C$190 million at time zero.
  - Cash flows of C$40 million per year for Years 1–10 if demand is "high."
  - Cash flows of C$20 million per year for Years 1–10 if demand is "low."
- Additional cash flows with the optional expansion project:
  - An outlay of C$190 million at time one.
  - Cash flows of C$40 million per year for Years 2–10 if demand is "high."
  - Cash flows of C$20 million per year for Years 2–10 if demand is "low."
- Whether demand is "high" or "low" in Years 1–10 will be revealed during the first year. The probability of "high" demand is 0.50, and the probably of "low" demand is 0.50.
- The option to make the expansion investment depends on making the initial investment. If the initial investment is not made, the option to expand does not exist.
- The required rate of return is 10 percent.

Society Services wants to evaluate its investment alternatives.

The internal auditor for Laroche Industries has made several suggestions for improving capital budgeting processes at the company. The internal auditor's suggestions are as follows:

Suggestion 1.   "In order to put all capital budgeting proposals on an equal footing, the projects should all use the risk-free rate for the required rate of return."

Suggestion 2.   "Because you cannot exercise both of them, you should not permit a given project to have both an abandonment option and an expansion/growth option."

Suggestion 3.   "When rationing capital, it is better to choose the portfolio of investments that maximizes the company NPV than the portfolio that maximizes the company IRR."

Suggestion 4.   "Project betas should be used for establishing the required rate of return whenever the project's beta is different from the company's beta."

33. What is the optimal service life for Laroche Livery's fleet of vans?
    A. Two years.
    B. Three years.
    C. Four years.

34. The optimal subset of the six projects that Schoeman is considering consists of Projects:
    A. 1 and 5.
    B. 2, 3, and 4.
    C. 2, 4, 5, and 6.

35. What is the NPV (C$ millions) of the original project for Society Services without considering the expansion option?
    A. −6.11.
    B. −5.66.
    C. 2.33.

36. What is the NPV (C$ millions) of the optimal set of investment decisions for Society Services including the expansion option?
    A. 6.34.
    B. 12.68.
    C. 31.03.

37. Should the capital budgeting committee accept the internal auditor's first and second suggestions, respectively?
    A. No for Suggestions 1 and 2.
    B. No for Suggestion 1 and Yes for Suggestion 2.
    C. Yes for Suggestion 1 and No for Suggestion 2.

38. Should the capital budgeting committee accept the internal auditor's third and fourth suggestions, respectively?
    A. No for Suggestions 3 and 4.
    B. Yes for Suggestions 3 and 4.
    C. No for Suggestion 3 and Yes for Suggestion 4.

The following information relates to Questions 39–44.

Maximilian Böhm is reviewing several capital budgeting proposals from subsidiaries of his company. Although his reviews deal with several details that may seem like minutiae, the company places a premium on the care it exercises in making its investment decisions.

The first proposal is a project for Richie Express, which is investing $500,000, all in fixed capital, in a project that will have depreciation and operating income after taxes, respectively, of $40,000 and $20,000 each year for the next three years. Richie Express will sell the asset in three years, paying 30 percent taxes on any excess of the selling price over book value. The proposal indicates that a $647,500 terminal selling price will enable the company to earn a 15 percent internal rate of return on the investment. Böhm doubts that this terminal value estimate is correct.

Another proposal concerns Gasup Company, which does natural gas exploration. A new investment has been identified by the Gasup finance department with the following projected cash flows:

- Investment outlays are $6 million immediately and $1 million at the end of the first year.
- After-tax operating cash flows are $0.5 million at the end of the first year and $4 million at the end of each of the second, third, fourth, and fifth years. In addition, an after-tax outflow occurs at the end of the five-year project that has not been included in the operating cash flows: $5 million required for environmental cleanup.
- The required rate of return on natural gas exploration is 18 percent.

The Gasup analyst is unsure about the calculation of the NPV and the IRR because the outlay is staged over two years.

Finally, Dominion Company is evaluating two mutually exclusive projects: The Pinto grinder involves an outlay of $100,000, annual after-tax operating cash flows of $45,000, an after-tax salvage value of $25,000, and a three-year life. The Bolten grinder has an outlay of $125,000, annual after-tax operating cash flows of $47,000, an after-tax salvage value of $20,000, and a four-year life. The required rate of return is 10 percent. The net present value (NPV) and equivalent annual annuity (EAA) of the Pinto grinder are $30,691 and $12,341, respectively. Whichever grinder is chosen, it will have to be replaced at the end of its service life. The analyst is unsure about which grinder should be chosen.

Böhm and his colleague Beth Goldberg have an extended conversation about capital budgeting issues, including several comments listed below. Goldberg makes two comments about real options:

1. "The abandonment option is valuable, but it should be exercised only when the abandonment value is above the amount of the original investment."
2. "If the cost of a real option is less than its value, this will increase the NPV of the investment project in which the real option is embedded."

Böhm also makes several comments about specific projects under consideration:

A. "The land and building were purchased five years ago for $10 million. This is the amount that should now be included in the fixed capital investment."
B. "We can improve the project's NPV by using the after-tax cost of debt as the discount rate. If we finance the project with 100 percent debt, this discount rate would be appropriate."
C. "It is generally safer to use the NPV than the IRR in making capital budgeting decisions. However, when evaluating mutually exclusive projects, if the projects have conventional cash flow patterns and have the same investment outlays, it is acceptable to use either the NPV or IRR."
D. "You should not base a capital budgeting decision on its immediate impact on earnings per share (EPS)."

39. What terminal selling price is required for a 15% internal rate of return on the Richie project?
    A. $588,028.
    B. $593,771.
    C. $625,839.

40. The NPV and IRR, respectively, of the Gasup Company investment are *closest* to:
    A. $509,600 and 21.4%.
    B. $509,600 and 31.3%.
    C. $946,700 and 31.3%.

41. Of the two grinders that the Dominion Company is evaluating, Böhm should recommend the:
    A. Bolten grinder because its NPV is higher than the Pinto grinder NPV.
    B. Bolten grinder because its EAA is higher than the Pinto grinder EAA.
    C. Pinto grinder because its EAA is higher than the Bolten grinder EAA.

42. Are Goldberg's comments about real options correct?
    A. No for Comment #1 and Comment #2.
    B. No for Comment #1 and Yes for Comment #2.
    C. Yes for Comment #1 and No for Comment #2.

43. Is Böhm most likely correct regarding Comment A about the $10 million investment and Comment B about using the after-tax cost of debt?
    A. No for both comments.
    B. Yes for both comments.
    C. No for Comment A and Yes for Comment B

44. Is Böhm most likely correct regarding Comment C that it is acceptable to use either NPV or IRR and Comment D about the immediate impact on EPS?
    A. No for both comments.
    B. Yes for both comments.
    C. No for Comment C and Yes for Comment D.

The following information relates to Questions 45–50.

Barbara Simpson is a sell-side analyst with Smith Riccardi Securities. Simpson covers the pharmaceutical industry. One of the companies she follows, Bayonne Pharma, is evaluating a regional distribution center. The financial predictions for the project are as follows:

- Fixed capital outlay is €1.50 billion.
- Investment in net working capital is €0.40 billion.
- Straight-line depreciation is over a six-year period with zero salvage value.
- Project life is 12 years.
- Additional annual revenues are €0.10 billion.
- Annual cash operating expenses are reduced by €0.25 billion.
- The capital equipment is sold for €0.50 billion in 12 years.
- Tax rate is 40 percent.
- Required rate of return is 12 percent.

Simpson is evaluating this investment to see whether it has the potential to affect Bayonne Pharma's stock price. Simpson estimates the NPV of the project to be €0.41 billion, which should increase the value of the company.

Simpson is evaluating the effects of other changes to her capital budgeting assumptions. She wants to know the effect of a switch from straight-line to accelerated depreciation on the company's operating income and the project's NPV. She also believes that the initial outlay might be much smaller than initially assumed. Specifically, she thinks the outlay for fixed capital might be €0.24 billion lower, with no change in salvage value.

When reviewing her work, Simpson's supervisor provides the following comments. "I note that you are relying heavily on the NPV approach to valuing the investment decision. I don't think you should use an IRR because of the multiple IRR problem that is likely to arise with the Bayonne Pharma project. However, the equivalent annual annuity would be a more appropriate measure to use for the project than the NPV. I suggest that you compute an EAA."

45. Simpson should estimate the after-tax operating cash flow for Years 1–6 and 7–12, respectively, to be *closest* to:
    A. €0.31 billion and €0.21 billion.
    B. €0.31 billion and €0.25 billion.
    C. €0.35 billion and €0.25 billion.

46. Simpson should estimate the initial outlay and the terminal year nonoperating cash flow, respectively, to be *closest* to:
    A. €1.50 billion and €0.70 billion.
    B. €1.90 billion and €0.70 billion.
    C. €1.90 billion and €0.90 billion.

47. Is Simpson's estimate of the NPV of the project correct?
    A. Yes.
    B. No. The NPV is –€0.01 billion.
    C. No. The NPV is €0.34 billion.

48. A switch from straight-line to accelerated depreciation would:
    A. increase the NPV and decrease the first year operating income after taxes.
    B. increase the first year operating income after taxes and decrease the NPV.
    C. increase both the NPV and first year operating income after taxes.

49. If the outlay is lower by the amount that Simpson suggests, the project NPV should increase by an amount *closest* to:
    A. €0.09 billion.
    B. €0.14 billion.
    C. €0.17 billion.

50. How would you evaluate the comments by Simpson's supervisor about not using the IRR and about using the EAA? The supervisor is:
    A. incorrect about both.
    B. correct about IRR and incorrect about EAA.
    C. incorrect about IRR and correct about EAA.

The following information relates to Questions 51–56.

Mun Hoe Yip is valuing Pure Corporation. Pure is a simple corporation that is going out of business in five years, distributing its income to creditors and bondholders as planned in the financial statements below. Pure has a 19 percent cost of equity, $8\frac{1}{3}$ percent before-tax cost of debt, 12 percent weighted average cost of capital, and 40 percent tax rate, and it maintains a 50 percent debt/value ratio.

Yip is valuing the company using the basic capital budgeting method as well as other methods, such as EP, residual income, and claims valuation. Yip's research assistant, Linda Robinson, makes three observations about the analysis.

Observation 1:	"The present value of the company's economic income should be equal to the present value of the cash flows in the basic capital budgeting approach."
Observation 2:	"The economic income each year is equal to the cash flow minus the economic depreciation."
Observation 3:	"The market value added is the present value of the company's economic profit (EP), which equals the net worth of 77,973."

Year	0	1	2	3	4	5
Balance Sheets:						
Assets	200,000	160,000	120,000	80,000	40,000	0
Liabilities	122,027	107,671	88,591	64,222	33,929	0
Net worth	77,973	52,329	31,409	15,778	6,071	0
Income Statements:						
Sales		180,000	200,000	220,000	240,000	200,000
Variable cash expenses		90,000	100,000	110,000	120,000	100,000
Fixed cash expenses		20,000	20,000	20,000	20,000	20,000
Depreciation		40,000	40,000	40,000	40,000	40,000
EBIT		30,000	40,000	50,000	60,000	40,000
Interest expense		10,169	8,973	7,383	5,352	2,827
EBT		19,831	31,027	42,617	54,648	37,173
Taxes at 40 percent		7,932	12,411	17,047	21,859	14,869
Net income before salvage		11,899	18,616	25,570	32,789	22,304
After-tax salvage value						12,000
Net income		11,899	18,616	25,570	32,789	34,304
Statements of Cash Flows:						
Operating cash flows:						
Net income		11,899	18,616	25,570	32,789	34,304
Depreciation		40,000	40,000	40,000	40,000	40,000
Total		51,899	58,616	65,570	72,789	74,304

Year	0	1	2	3	4	5
Financing cash flows:						
Debt repayment		14,357	19,080	24,369	30,293	33,929
Dividends/repurchases		37,542	39,536	41,201	42,496	40,375
Total		−51,899	−58,616	−65,570	−72,789	−74,304
Investing cash flows:	0	0	0	0	0	0
Total cash flows:	0	0	0	0	0	0

51. Economic income during Year 1 is *closest* to:
    A. 23,186.
    B. 29,287.
    C. 46,101.

52. What is EP during Year 1?
    A. −12,101.
    B. −6,000.
    C. 6,000.

53. What is residual income during Year 1?
    A. −2,916.
    B. 2,542.
    C. 8,653.

54. What is the value of equity at time zero?
    A. 44,055.
    B. 77,973.
    C. 122,027.

55. Are Robinson's first two observations, respectively, correct?
    A. Yes for both observations.
    B. No for the first and Yes for the second.
    C. Yes for the first and No for the second.

56. Which of the following would be Yip's *most* appropriate response to Robinson's third observation?
    A. The market value added is not equal to the present value of EP, although the market value of equity is equal to 122,027.
    B. The market value added is equal to the present value of EP, which in this case is 44,055.
    C. The market value added is not equal to the present value of EP, and market value added is equal to 44,055.

CHAPTER 3

COST OF CAPITAL

LEARNING OUTCOMES

After completing this chapter, you will be able to do the following:

- Calculate and interpret the weighted average cost of capital (WACC) of a company.
- Describe how taxes affect the cost of capital from different capital sources.
- Explain alternative methods of calculating the weights used in the WACC, including the use of the company's target capital structure.
- Explain how the marginal cost of capital and the investment opportunity schedule are used to determine the optimal capital budget.
- Explain the marginal cost of capital's role in determining the net present value of a project.
- Calculate and interpret the cost of fixed rate debt capital using the yield-to-maturity approach and the debt-rating approach.
- Calculate and interpret the cost of noncallable, nonconvertible preferred stock.
- Calculate and interpret the cost of equity capital using the capital asset pricing model approach, the dividend discount approach, and the bond yield plus risk premium approach.
- Calculate and interpret the beta and cost of capital for a project.
- Explain the country equity risk premium in the estimation of the cost of equity for a company located in a developing market.
- Describe the marginal cost of capital schedule, explain why it may be upward sloping with respect to additional capital, and calculate and interpret its break points.
- Explain and demonstrate the correct treatment of flotation costs.

SUMMARY OVERVIEW

- The weighted average cost of capital is a weighted average of the after-tax marginal costs of each source of capital: $WACC = w_d r_d (1 - t) + w_p r_p + w_e r_e$.
- An analyst uses the WACC in valuation. For example, the WACC is used to value a project using the net present value method: $NPV = $ Present value of inflows $-$ Present value of the outflows.
- The before-tax cost of debt is generally estimated by means of one of the two methods: yield to maturity or bond rating.

- The yield-to-maturity method of estimating the before-tax cost of debt uses the familiar bond valuation equation. Assuming semiannual coupon payments, the equation is

$$P_0 = \frac{PMT_1}{\left(1 + \frac{r_d}{2}\right)} + \cdots + \frac{PMT_n}{\left(1 + \frac{r_d}{2}\right)^n} + \frac{FV}{\left(1 + \frac{r_d}{2}\right)^n} = \left(\sum_{t=1}^{n} \frac{PMT_t}{\left(1 + \frac{r_d}{2}\right)^t}\right) + \frac{FV}{\left(1 + \frac{r_d}{2}\right)^n}$$

   We solve for the six-month yield ($r_d/2$) and then annualize it to arrive at the before-tax cost of debt, r_d.
- Because interest payments are generally tax deductible, the after-tax cost is the true, effective cost of debt to the company. If a current yield or bond rating is not available, such as in the case of a private company without rated debt or a project, the estimate of the cost of debt becomes more challenging.
- The cost of preferred stock is the preferred stock dividend divided by the current preferred stock price:

$$r_p = \frac{D_p}{P_p}$$

- The cost of equity is the rate of return required by a company's common stockholders. We estimate this cost using the CAPM (or its variants) or the dividend discount method.
- The CAPM is the approach most commonly used to calculate the cost of common stock. The three components needed to calculate the cost of common stock are the risk-free rate, the equity risk premium, and beta:

$$E(R_i) = R_F + \beta_i[E(R_M) - R_F]$$

- When estimating the cost of equity capital using the CAPM when we do not have publicly traded equity, we may be able to use the pure-play method in which we estimate the unlevered beta for a company with similar business risk, β_U,

$$\beta_{U,\text{comparable}} = \frac{\beta_{L,\text{comparable}}}{\left[1 + \left((1 - t_{\text{comparable}})\dfrac{D_{\text{comparable}}}{E_{\text{comparable}}}\right)\right]}$$

   and then lever this beta to reflect the financial risk of the project or company:

$$\beta_{L,\text{project}} = \beta_{U,\text{comparable}}\left[1 + \left((1 - t_{\text{project}})\dfrac{D_{\text{project}}}{E_{\text{project}}}\right)\right]$$

- It is often the case that country and foreign exchange risk are diversified so that we can use the estimated β in the CAPM analysis. However, in the case in which these risks cannot be diversified away, we can adjust our measure of systematic risk by a country equity premium to reflect this nondiversified risk:

$$\text{Country equity premium} = \text{Sovereign yield spread} \left(\frac{\text{Annualized standard deviation of equity index}}{\begin{array}{c}\text{Annualized standard deviation of the}\\\text{sovereign bond market in terms}\\\text{of the developed market currency}\end{array}} \right)$$

- The dividend discount model approach is an alternative approach to calculating the cost of equity, whereby the cost of equity is estimated as follows:

$$r_e = \frac{D_1}{P_0} + g$$

- We can estimate the growth rate in the dividend discount model by using published forecasts of analysts or by estimating the sustainable growth rate:

$$g = (1 - D/\text{EPS})\,\text{ROE}$$

- In estimating the cost of equity, an alternative to the CAPM and dividend discount approaches is the bond yield plus risk premium approach. In this approach, we estimate the before-tax cost of debt and add a risk premium that reflects the additional risk associated with the company's equity.
- The marginal cost of capital schedule is a graph plotting the new funds raised by a company on the *x*-axis and the cost of capital on the *y*-axis. The cost of capital is level to the point at which one of the costs of capital changes, such as when the company bumps up against a debt covenant, requiring it to use another form of capital. We calculate a break point using information on when the different sources' costs change and the proportions that the company uses when it raises additional capital:

$$\text{Break point} = \frac{\text{Amount of capital at which the source's cost of capital changes}}{\text{Proportion of new capital raised from the source}}$$

- Flotation costs are costs incurred in the process of raising additional capital. The preferred method of including these costs in the analysis is as an initial cash flow in the valuation analysis.
- Survey evidence tells us that the CAPM method is the most popular method used by companies in estimating the cost of equity. The CAPM is more popular with larger, publicly traded companies, which is understandable considering the additional analyses and assumptions required in estimating systematic risk for a private company or project.

PROBLEMS

1. The cost of equity is equal to the:
   A. expected market return.
   B. rate of return required by stockholders.
   C. cost of retained earnings plus dividends.

2. Which of the following statements is correct?
    A. The appropriate tax rate to use in the adjustment of the before-tax cost of debt to determine the after-tax cost of debt is the average tax rate because interest is deductible against the company's entire taxable income.
    B. For a given company, the after-tax cost of debt is generally less than both the cost of preferred equity and the cost of common equity.
    C. For a given company, the investment opportunity schedule is upward sloping because as a company invests more in capital projects, the returns from investing increase.

3. Using the dividend discount model, what is the cost of equity capital for Zeller Mining if the company will pay a dividend of C$2.30 next year, has a payout ratio of 30%, a return on equity (ROE) of 15%, and a stock price of C$45?
    A. 9.61%.
    B. 10.50%.
    C. 15.61%.

4. Dot.Com has determined that it could issue $1,000 face value bonds with an 8% coupon paid semiannually and a five-year maturity at $900 per bond. If Dot.Com's marginal tax rate is 38%, its after-tax cost of debt is *closest* to:
    A. 6.2%.
    B. 6.4%.
    C. 6.6%.

5. The cost of debt can be determined using the yield-to-maturity and the bond rating approaches. If the bond rating approach is used, the:
    A. coupon is the yield.
    B. yield is based on the interest coverage ratio.
    C. company is rated and the rating can be used to assess the credit default spread of the company's debt.

6. Morgan Insurance Ltd. issued a fixed-rate perpetual preferred stock three years ago and placed it privately with institutional investors. The stock was issued at $25 per share with a $1.75 dividend. If the company were to issue preferred stock today, the yield would be 6.5%. The stock's current value is:
    A. $25.00.
    B. $26.92.
    C. $37.31.

7. A financial analyst at Buckco Ltd. wants to compute the company's weighted average cost of capital (WACC) using the dividend discount model. The analyst has gathered the following data:

Before-tax cost of new debt	8%
Tax rate	40%
Target debt-to-equity ratio	0.8033
Stock price	$30
Next year's dividend	$1.50
Estimated growth rate	7%

Buckco's WACC is *closest* to:
A. 8%.
B. 9%.
C. 12%.

8. The Gearing Company has an after-tax cost of debt capital of 4%, a cost of preferred stock of 8%, a cost of equity capital of 10%, and a weighted average cost of capital of 7%. Gearing intends to maintain its current capital structure as it raises additional capital. In making its capital-budgeting decisions for the average-risk project, the relevant cost of capital is:
A. 4%.
B. 7%.
C. 8%.

9. Fran McClure of Alba Advisers is estimating the cost of capital of Frontier Corporation as part of her valuation analysis of Frontier. McClure will be using this estimate, along with projected cash flows from Frontier's new projects, to estimate the effect of these new projects on the value of Frontier. McClure has gathered the following information on Frontier Corporation:

	Current Year	Forecasted for Next Year
Book value of debt	$50	$50
Market value of debt	$62	$63
Book value of shareholders' equity	$55	$58
Market value of shareholders' equity	$210	$220

The weights that McClure should apply in estimating Frontier's cost of capital for debt and equity are, respectively:
A. $w_d = 0.200$; $w_e = 0.800$.
B. $w_d = 0.185$; $w_e = 0.815$.
C. $w_d = 0.223$; $w_e = 0.777$.

10. Wang Securities had a long-term stable debt-to-equity ratio of 0.65. Recent bank borrowing for expansion into South America raised the ratio to 0.75. The increased leverage has what effect on the asset beta and equity beta of the company?
A. The asset beta and the equity beta will both rise.
B. The asset beta will remain the same and the equity beta will rise.
C. The asset beta will remain the same and the equity beta will decline.

11. Brandon Wiene is a financial analyst covering the beverage industry. He is evaluating the impact of DEF Beverage's new product line of flavored waters. DEF currently has a debt-to-equity ratio of 0.6. The new product line would be financed with $50 million of debt and $100 million of equity. In estimating the valuation impact of this new product line on DEF's value, Wiene has estimated the equity beta and asset beta of comparable companies. In calculating the equity beta for the product line, Wiene is intending to use DEF's existing capital structure when converting the asset beta into a project beta. Which of the following statements is correct?

A. Using DEF's debt-to-equity ratio of 0.6 is appropriate in calculating the new product line's equity beta.
B. Using DEF's debt-to-equity ratio of 0.6 is not appropriate, but rather the debt-to-equity ratio of the new product, 0.5, is appropriate to use in calculating the new product line's equity beta.
C. Wiene should use the new debt-to-equity ratio of DEF that would result from the additional $50 million debt and $100 million equity in calculating the new product line's equity beta.

12. Trumpit Resorts Company currently has 1.2 million common shares of stock outstanding and the stock has a beta of 2.2. It also has $10 million face value of bonds that have five years remaining to maturity and 8% coupon with semiannual payments, and are priced to yield 13.65%. If Trumpit issues up to $2.5 million of new bonds, the bonds will be priced at par and have a yield of 13.65%; if it issues bonds beyond $2.5 million, the expected yield on the entire issuance will be 16%. Trumpit has learned that it can issue new common stock at $10 a share. The current risk-free rate of interest is 3% and the expected market return is 10%. Trumpit's marginal tax rate is 30%. If Trumpit raises $7.5 million of new capital while maintaining the same debt-to-equity ratio, its weighted average cost of capital is *closest* to:
A. 14.5%.
B. 15.5%.
C. 16.5%.

The following information relates to Questions 13–18.

Jurgen Knudsen has been hired to provide industry expertise to Henrik Sandell, CFA, an analyst for a pension plan managing a global large-cap fund internally. Sandell is concerned about one of the fund's larger holdings, auto parts manufacturer Kruspa AB. Kruspa currently operates in 80 countries, with the previous year's global revenues at €5.6 billion. Recently, Kruspa's CFO announced plans for expansion into China. Sandell worries that this expansion will change the company's risk profile and wonders if he should recommend a sale of the position.

Sandell provides Knudsen with the basic information. Kruspa's global annual free cash flow to the firm is €500 million and earnings are €400 million. Sandell estimates that cash flow will level off at a 2 percent rate of growth. Sandell also estimates that Kruspa's after-tax free cash flow to the firm on the China project for next three years is, respectively, €48 million, €52 million, and €54.4 million. Kruspa recently announced a dividend of €4.00 per share of stock. For the initial analysis, Sandell requests that Knudsen ignore possible currency fluctuations. He expects the Chinese plant to sell only to customers within China for the first three years. Knudsen is asked to evaluate Kruspa's planned financing of the required €100 million with a €80 public offering of 10-year debt in Sweden and the remainder with an equity offering.
Additional information:

Equity risk premium, Sweden	4.82%
Risk-free rate of interest, Sweden	4.25%
Industry debt-to-equity ratio	0.3
Market value of Kruspa's debt	€900 million
Market value of Kruspa's equity	€2.4 billion

Kruspa's equity beta	1.3
Kruspa's before-tax cost of debt	9.25%
China credit A2 country risk premium	1.88%
Corporate tax rate	37.5%
Interest payments each year	Level

13. Using the capital asset pricing model, Kruspa's cost of equity capital for its typical project is *closest* to:
    A. 7.62%.
    B. 10.52%.
    C. 12.40%.

14. Sandell is interested in the weighted average cost of capital of Kruspa AB prior to its investing in the China project. This weighted average cost of capital (WACC) is *closest* to:
    A. 7.65%.
    B. 9.23%.
    C. 10.17%.

15. In his estimation of the project's cost of capital, Sandell would like to use the asset beta of Kruspa as a base in his calculations. The estimated asset beta of Kruspa prior to the China project is *closest* to:
    A. 1.053.
    B. 1.110.
    C. 1.327.

16. Sandell is performing a sensitivity analysis of the effect of the new project on the company's cost of capital. If the China project has the same asset risk as Kruspa, the estimated project beta for the China project, if it is financed 80% with debt, is *closest* to:
    A. 1.300.
    B. 2.635.
    C. 3.686.

17. As part of the sensitivity analysis of the effect of the new project on the company's cost of capital, Sandell is estimating the cost of equity of the China project considering that the China project requires a country equity premium to capture the risk of the project. The cost of equity for the project in this case is *closest* to:
    A. 10.52%.
    B. 19.91%.
    C. 28.95%.

18. In his report, Sandell would like to discuss the sensitivity of the project's net present value to the estimation of the cost of equity. The China project's net present value calculated using the equity beta without and with the country risk premium are, respectively:
    A. €26 million and €24 million.
    B. €28 million and €25 million.
    C. €30 million and €27 million.

The following information relates to Questions 19–22.

Boris Duarte, CFA, covers initial public offerings for Zellweger Analytics, an independent research firm specializing in global small-cap equities. He has been asked to evaluate the upcoming new issue of TagOn, a U.S.-based business intelligence software company. The industry has grown at 26 percent per year for the previous three years. Large companies dominate the market, but sizable "pure-play" companies such as Relevant, Ltd., ABJ, Inc., and Opus Software Pvt. Ltd also compete. Each of these competitors is domiciled in a different country, but they all have shares of stock that trade on the U.S. NASDAQ. The debt ratio of the industry has risen slightly in recent years.

Company	Sales (in millions)	Market Value Equity (in millions)	Market Value Debt (in millions)	Equity Beta	Tax Rate	Share Price
Relevant Ltd.	$752	$3,800	$0.0	1.702	23%	$42
ABJ, Inc.	$843	$2,150	$6.5	2.800	23%	$24
Opus Software Pvt. Ltd.	$211	$972	$13.0	3.400	23%	$13

Duarte uses the information from the preliminary prospectus for TagOn's initial offering. The company intends to issue 1 million new shares. In his conversation with the investment bankers for the deal, he concludes the offering price will be between $7 and $12. The current capital structure of TagOn consists of a $2.4 million five-year noncallable bond issue and 1 million common shares. Other information that Duarte has gathered:

Currently outstanding bonds	$2.4 million five-year bonds, coupon of 12.5 percent, with a market value of $2.156 million
Risk-free rate of interest	5.25%
Estimated equity risk premium	7%
Tax rate	23%

19. The asset betas for Relevant, ABJ, and Opus, respectively, are:
    A. 1.70, 2.52, and 2.73.
    B. 1.70, 2.79, and 3.37.
    C. 1.70, 2.81, and 3.44.

20. The average asset beta for the pure players in this industry, Relevant, ABJ, and Opus, weighted by market value of equity is *closest* to:
    A. 1.67.
    B. 1.97.
    C. 2.27.

21. Using the capital asset pricing model, the cost of equity capital for a company in this industry with a debt-to-equity ratio of 0.01, asset beta of 2.27, and a marginal tax rate of 23% is *closest* to:

A. 17%.
B. 21%.
C. 24%.

22. The marginal cost of capital for TagOn, based on an average asset beta of 2.27 for the industry and assuming that new stock can be issued at $8 per share, is *closest* to:
A. 20.5%.
B. 21.0%.
C. 21.5%.

23. Two years ago, a company issued $20 million in long-term bonds at par value with a coupon rate of 9%. The company has decided to issue an additional $20 million in bonds and expects the new issue to be priced at par value with a coupon rate of 7%. The company has no other debt outstanding and has a tax rate of 40%. To compute the company's weighted average cost of capital, the appropriate after-tax cost of debt is *closest* to:
A. 4.2%.
B. 4.8%.
C. 5.4%.

24. An analyst gathered the following information about a company and the market:

Current market price per share of common stock	$28.00
Most recent dividend per share paid on common stock (D_0)	$2.00
Expected dividend payout rate	40%
Expected return on equity (ROE)	15%
Beta for the common stock	1.3
Expected rate of return on the market portfolio	13%
Risk-free rate of return	4%

Using the discounted cash flow (DCF) approach, the cost of retained earnings for the company is *closest* to:
A. 15.7%.
B. 16.1%.
C. 16.8%.

25. An analyst gathered the following information about a company and the market:

Current market price per share of common stock	$28.00
Most recent dividend per share paid on common stock (D_0)	$2.00
Expected dividend payout rate	40%
Expected return on equity (ROE)	15%
Beta for the common stock	1.3
Expected rate of return on the market portfolio	13%
Risk-free rate of return	4%

Using the capital asset pricing model (CAPM) approach, the cost of retained earnings for the company is *closest* to:

A. 13.6%.

B. 15.7%.

C. 16.1%.

26. An analyst gathered the following information about a private company and its publicly traded competitor:

Comparable Companies	Tax Rate	Debt/Equity	Equity Beta
Private company	30.0%	1.00	N.A.
Public company	35.0%	0.90	1.75

Using the pure-play method, the estimated equity beta for the private company is *closest* to:

A. 1.029.

B. 1.104.

C. 1.877.

27. An analyst gathered the following information about the capital markets in the United States and in Paragon, a developing country.

Selected Market Information	
Yield on U.S. 10-year Treasury bond	4.5%
Yield on Paragon 10-year government bond	10.5%
Annualized standard deviation of Paragon stock index	35.0%
Annualized standard deviation of Paragon dollar-denominated government bond	25.0%

Based on the analyst's data, the estimated country equity premium for Paragon is *closest* to:

A. 4.29%.

B. 6.00%.

C. 8.40%.

CHAPTER 4

MEASURES OF LEVERAGE

LEARNING OUTCOMES

After completing this chapter, you will be able to do the following:

- Define and explain leverage, business risk, sales risk, operating risk, and financial risk and classify a risk, given a description.
- Calculate and interpret the degree of operating leverage, the degree of financial leverage, and the degree of total leverage.
- Describe the effect of financial leverage on a company's net income and return on equity.
- Calculate the breakeven quantity of sales and determine the company's net income at various sales levels.
- Calculate and interpret the operating breakeven quantity of sales.

SUMMARY OVERVIEW

- Leverage is the use of fixed costs in a company's cost structure. Business risk is the risk associated with operating earnings and reflects both sales risk (uncertainty with respect to the price and quantity of sales) and operating risk (the risk related to the use of fixed costs in operations). Financial risk is the risk associated with how a company finances its operations (i.e., the split between equity and debt financing of the business).
- The degree of operating leverage (DOL) is the ratio of the percentage change in operating income to the percentage change in units sold. We can use the following formula to measure the degree of operating leverage:

$$\text{DOL} = \frac{Q(P - V)}{Q(P - V) - F}$$

- The degree of financial leverage (DFL) is the percentage change in net income for a given percentage change in operating income. We can use the following formula to measure the degree of financial leverage:

$$\text{DFL} = \frac{[Q(P - V) - F](1 - t)}{[Q(P - V) - F - C](1 - t)} = \frac{[Q(P - V) - F]}{[Q(P - V) - F - C]}$$

- The degree of total leverage (DTL) is a measure of the sensitivity of the cash flows to owners to changes in unit sales, which is equivalent to $DTL = DOL \times DFL$.
- The breakeven point, Q_{BE}, is the number of units produced and sold at which the company's net income is zero, which we calculate as

$$Q_{BE} = \frac{F + C}{P - V}$$

- The operating breakeven point, Q_{OBE}, is the number of units produced and sold at which the company's operating income is zero, which we calculate as

$$Q_{OBE} = \frac{F}{P - V}$$

PROBLEMS

1. If two companies have identical unit sales volume and operating risk, they are *most likely* to also have identical:
   A. sales risk.
   B. business risk.
   C. sensitivity of operating earnings to changes in the number of units produced and sold.

2. Degree of operating leverage is *best* described as a measure of the sensitivity of:
   A. net earnings to changes in sales.
   B. fixed operating costs to changes in variable costs.
   C. operating earnings to changes in the number of units produced and sold.

3. The Fulcrum Company produces decorative swivel platforms for home televisions. If Fulcrum produces 40 million units, it estimates that it can sell them for $100 each. Variable production costs are $65 per unit and fixed production costs are $1.05 billion. Which of the following statements is *most* accurate? Holding all else constant, the Fulcrum Company would:
   A. generate positive operating income if unit sales were 25 million.
   B. have less operating leverage if fixed production costs were 10% greater than $1.05 billion.
   C. generate 20% more operating income if unit sales were 5% greater than 40 million.

4. The business risk of a particular company is *most* accurately measured by the company's:
   A. debt-to-equity ratio.
   B. efficiency in using assets to generate sales.
   C. operating leverage and level of uncertainty about demand, output prices, and competition.

5. Consider two companies that operate in the same line of business and have the same degree of operating leverage: the Basic Company and the Grundlegend Company. The Basic Company and the Grundlegend Company have, respectively, no debt and 50 percent debt in their capital structure. Which of the following statements is *most* accurate? Compared to the Basic Company, the Grundlegend Company has:

   A. a lower sensitivity of net income to changes in unit sales.

   B. the same sensitivity of operating income to changes in unit sales.

   C. the same sensitivity of net income to changes in operating income.

6. Myundia Motors now sells 1 million units at ¥3,529 per unit. Fixed operating costs are ¥1,290 million and variable operating costs are ¥1,500 per unit. If the company pays ¥410 million in interest, the levels of sales at the operating breakeven and breakeven points are, respectively:

   A. ¥1,500,000,000 and ¥2,257,612,900.

   B. ¥2,243,671,760 and ¥2,956,776,737.

   C. ¥2,975,148,800 and ¥3,529,000,000.

7. Juan Alavanca is evaluating the risk of two companies in the machinery industry: The Gearing Company and Hebelkraft, Inc. Alavanca used the latest fiscal year's financial statements and interviews with managers of the respective companies to gather the following information:

	The Gearing Company	Hebelkraft, Inc.
Number of units produced and sold	1 million	1.5 million
Sales price per unit	$200	$200
Variable cost per unit	$120	$100
Fixed operating cost	$40 million	$90 million
Fixed financing expense	$20 million	$20 million

Based on this information, the breakeven points for The Gearing Company and Hebelkraft, Inc. are:

   A. 0.75 million and 1.1 million units, respectively.

   B. 1 million and 1.5 million units, respectively.

   C. 1.5 million and 0.75 million units, respectively.

The following information relates to Questions 8–16.[1]

Mary Benn, CFA, is a financial analyst for Twin Fields Investments, located in Storrs, Connecticut, U.S.A. She has been asked by her supervisor, Bill Cho, to examine two small Japanese cell phone component manufacturers: 4G, Inc. and Qphone Corp. Cho indicates that his clients are most interested in the use of leverage by 4G and Qphone. Benn states, "I will have to specifically analyze each company's respective business risk, sales risk, operating risk, and financial risk." "Fine, I'll check back with you shortly," Cho answers.

Benn begins her analysis by examining the sales prospects of the two firms. The results of her sales analysis appear in Exhibit A. She also expects very little price variability for these cell phones. She next gathers more data on these two companies to assist her analysis of their operating and financial risk.

---

[1] Questions developed by Philip Fanara, CFA.

When Cho inquires as to her progress, Benn responds, "I have calculated Qphone's degree of operating leverage (DOL) and degree of financial leverage (DFL) at Qphone's 2009 level of unit sales. I have also calculated Qphone's breakeven level for unit sales. I will have 4G's leverage results shortly."

Cho responds, "Good, I will call a meeting of some potential investors for tomorrow. Please help me explain these concepts to them, and the differences in use of leverage by these two companies." In preparation for the meeting, Cho says he has a number of questions:

- "You mentioned business risk; what is included in that?"
- "How would you classify the risk due to the varying mix of variable and fixed costs?"
- "Could you conduct an analysis and tell me how the two companies will fare relative to each other in terms of net income if their unit sales increased by 10 percent above their 2009 unit sales levels?"
- "Finally, what would be an accurate verbal description of the degree of total leverage?"

The relevant data for analysis of 4G is contained in Exhibit B, while Benn's analysis of the Qphone data appears in Exhibit C.

EXHIBIT A   Benn's Unit Sales Estimates for 4G, Inc., and Qphone Corp.

Company	2009 Unit Sales	Standard Deviation of Unit Sales	2010 Expected Unit Sales Growth Rate
4G, Inc.	1,000,000	25,000	15%
Qphone Corp.	1,500,000	10,000	15%

EXHIBIT B   Sales, Cost, and Expense Data for 4G, Inc. (At Unit Sales of 1,000,000)

Number of units produced and sold	1,000,000
Sales price per unit	¥108
Variable cost per unit	¥72
Fixed operating cost	¥22,500,000
Fixed financing expense	¥9,000,000

EXHIBIT C   Benn's Analysis of Qphone (At Unit Sales of 1,500,000)

Degree of operating leverage	1.40
Degree of financial leverage	1.15
Breakeven quantity (units)	571,429

8. Based on Benn's analysis, 4G's sales risk relative to Qphone's is *most likely* to be:
   A. lower.
   B. equal.
   C. higher.

9. What is the *most* appropriate response to Cho's question regarding the components of business risk?
   A. Sales risk and financial risk.
   B. Operating risk and sales risk.
   C. Financial risk and operating risk.

10. The *most* appropriate response to Cho's question regarding the classification of risk arising from the mixture of variable and fixed costs is:
    A. sales risk.
    B. financial risk.
    C. operating risk.

11. Based on the information in Exhibit B, the degree of operating leverage (DOL) of 4G, Inc., at unit sales of 1,000,000, is *closest* to:
    A. 1.60.
    B. 2.67.
    C. 3.20.

12. Based on the information in Exhibit B, 4G Inc.'s degree of financial leverage (DFL), at unit sales of 1,000,000, is *closest* to:
    A. 1.33.
    B. 2.67.
    C. 3.00.

13. Based on the information in Exhibit A and Exhibit C, Qphone's expected percentage change in operating income for 2010 is *closest* to:
    A. 17.25%.
    B. 21.00%.
    C. 24.30%.

14. 4G's breakeven quantity of unit sales is *closest* to:
    A. 437,500 units.
    B. 625,000 units.
    C. 875,000 units.

15. In response to Cho's question regarding an increase in unit sales above 2009 unit sales levels, it is *most likely* that 4G's net income will increase at:
    A. a slower rate than Qphone's.
    B. the same rate as Qphone's.
    C. a faster rate than Qphone's.

16. The *most* appropriate response to Cho's question regarding a description of the degree of total leverage is that degree of total leverage is:

    A. the percentage change in net income divided by the percentage change in units sold.

    B. the percentage change in operating income divided by the percentage change in units sold.

    C. the percentage change in net income divided by the percentage change in operating income.

CHAPTER 5

CAPITAL STRUCTURE

LEARNING OUTCOMES

After completing this chapter, you will be able to do the following:

- Explain the Modigliani–Miller propositions concerning capital structure, including the impact of leverage, taxes, financial distress, agency costs, and asymmetric information on a company's cost of equity, cost of capital, and optimal capital structure.
- Explain the target capital structure and why actual capital structure may fluctuate around the target.
- Describe the role of debt ratings in capital structure policy.
- Explain factors an analyst should consider in evaluating the impact of capital structure policy on valuation.
- Describe international differences in financial leverage and their implications for investment analysis.

SUMMARY OVERVIEW

- The goal of the capital structure decision is to determine the financial leverage that maximizes the value of the company (or minimizes the weighted average cost of capital).
- In the Modigliani and Miller theory developed without taxes, capital structure is irrelevant and has no effect on company value.
- The deductibility of interest lowers the cost of debt and the cost of capital for the company as a whole. Adding the tax shield provided by debt to the Modigliani and Miller framework suggests that the optimal capital structure is all debt.
- In the Modigliani and Miller propositions with and without taxes, increasing a company's relative use of debt in the capital structure increases the risk for equity providers and, hence, the cost of equity capital.
- When there are bankruptcy costs, a high debt ratio increases the risk of bankruptcy.
- Using more debt in a company's capital structure reduces the net agency costs of equity.
- The costs of asymmetric information increase as more equity is used versus debt, suggesting the pecking order theory of leverage, in which new equity issuance is the least preferred method of raising capital.
- According to the static trade-off theory of capital structure, in choosing a capital structure, a company balances the value of the tax benefit from deductibility of interest with the

present value of the costs of financial distress. At the optimal target capital structure, the incremental tax shield benefit is exactly offset by the incremental costs of financial distress.

- A company may identify its target capital structure, but its capital structure at any point in time may not be equal to its target for many reasons, including that management may exploit tactical opportunities in financing sources, market-value fluctuations in its securities, or just be unable to maintain the capital structure due to market conditions.

- Many companies have goals for maintaining a certain credit rating, and these goals are influenced by the relative costs of debt financing among the different rating classes.

- In evaluating a company's capital structure, the financial analyst must look at the capital structure of the company over time, the capital structure of competitors that have similar business risk, and company-specific factors, such as the quality of corporate governance, that may affect agency costs, among other factors.

- Good corporate governance and accounting transparency should lower the net agency costs of equity.

- When comparing capital structures of companies in different countries, an analyst must consider a variety of characteristics that might differ and affect both the typical capital structure and the debt maturity structure. The major characteristics fall into three categories: institutional and legal environment, financial markets and banking sector, and macro-economic environment.

PROBLEMS

1. If investors have homogeneous expectations, the market is efficient, and there are no taxes, no transactions costs, and no bankruptcy costs, the Modigliani and Miller Proposition I states that:
   A. bankruptcy risk rises with more leverage.
   B. managers cannot change the value of the company by using more or less debt.
   C. managers cannot increase the value of the company by employing tax saving strategies.

2. According to Modigliani and Miller's Proposition II without taxes:
   A. the capital structure decision has no effect on the cost of equity.
   B. investment and the capital structure decisions are interdependent.
   C. the cost of equity increases as the use of debt in the capital structure increases.

3. Suppose the weighted average cost of capital of the Gadget Company is 10%. If Gadget has a capital structure of 50% debt and 50% equity, a before-tax cost of debt of 5%, and a marginal tax rate of 20%, then its cost of equity capital is *closest* to:
   A. 12%.
   B. 14%.
   C. 16%.

4. The current weighted average cost of capital (WACC) for Van der Welde is 10%. The company announced a debt offering that raises the WACC to 13%. The *most likely* conclusion is that for Van der Welde:

    A. the company's prospects are improving.

    B. equity financing is cheaper than debt financing.

    C. the company's debt/equity ratio has moved beyond the optimal range.

5. All else equal, the use of long-maturity debt is expected to be greater in those markets in which:

    A. inflation is low.

    B. capital markets are passive and illiquid.

    C. the legal system's protection of bondholders' interests is weak.

6. According to the pecking order theory:

    A. new debt is preferable to new equity.

    B. new debt is preferable to internally generated funds.

    C. new equity is always preferable to other sources of capital.

7. According to the static trade-off theory:

    A. debt should be used only as a last resort.

    B. companies have an optimal level of debt.

    C. the capital structure decision is irrelevant.

The following information relates to Questions 8–13.

Barbara Andrade is an equity analyst who covers the entertainment industry for Greengable Capital Partners, a major global asset manager. Greengable owns a significant position with a large unrealized capital gain in Mosely Broadcast Group (MBG). On a recent conference call, MBG's management states that they plan to increase the proportion of debt in the company's capital structure. Andrade is concerned that any changes in MBG's capital structure will negatively affect the value of Greengable's investment.

To evaluate the potential impact of such a capital structure change on Greengable's investment, she gathers the information about MBG given in Exhibit A.

EXHIBIT A   Current Selected Financial Information for MBG

Yield to maturity on debt	8.00%
Market value of debt	$100 million
Number of shares of common stock	10 million
Market price per share of common stock	$30
Cost of capital if all equity-financed	10.3%
Marginal tax rate	35%

Andrade expects that an increase in MBG's financial leverage will increase its costs of debt and equity. Based on an examination of similar companies in MBG's industry, Andrade estimates MBG's cost of debt and cost of equity at various debt-to-total capital ratios, as shown in Exhibit B.

EXHIBIT B   Estimates of MBG's Before-Tax Costs of Debt
and Equity

Debt-to-Total Capital Ratio	Cost of Debt	Cost of Equity
20%	7.7%	12.5%
30%	8.4%	13.0%
40%	9.3%	14.0%
50%	10.4%	16.0%

8. MBG is *best* described as currently:
   A. 25% debt financed and 75% equity financed.
   B. 33% debt financed and 66% equity financed.
   C. 75% debt financed and 25% equity financed.

9. Based on Exhibits A and B, the current after-tax cost of debt for MBG is *closest* to:
   A. 2.80%.
   B. 5.20%.
   C. 7.65%.

10. Based on Exhibits A and B, MBG's current cost of equity capital is *closest* to:
    A. 10.30%.
    B. 10.80%.
    C. 12.75%.

11. Based on Exhibits A and B, what debt-to-total capital ratio would minimize MBG's weighted average cost of capital?
    A. 20%.
    B. 30%.
    C. 40%.

12. Holding operating earnings constant, an increase in the marginal tax rate to 40% would:
    A. result in a lower cost of debt capital.
    B. result in a higher cost of debt capital.
    C. not affect the company's cost of capital.

13. According to the pecking order theory, MBG's announced capital structure change:
    A. is optimal because debt is cheaper than equity on an after-tax basis.
    B. may be optimal if new debt is issued after new equity is made complete use of as a source of capital.
    C. may be optimal if new debt is issued after internally generated funds are made complete use of as a source of capital.

The following information relates to Questions 14–19.[1]

Lindsay White, CFA, is an analyst with a firm in London, England. She is responsible for covering five companies in the Consumer Staples industry. White believes the domestic and global economies will grow slightly below average over the next two years, but she is also concerned about the possibility of a mild recession taking hold. She has been asked to review the companies that she covers and has collected information about them, presented in Exhibit C. White has estimated that earnings before interest and taxes (EBIT) will remain constant for all five companies for the foreseeable future. Currency is in terms of the British pound (£). The marginal corporate tax rate is 30 percent for all five companies.

EXHIBIT C   Selected Company Financial Data

	Aquarius	Bema	Garth	Holte	Vega
EBIT (£)	600,000	600,000	400,000	400,000	400,000
Debt-to-equity ratio (market value)	0.60	0.00	0.00	0.71	0.62
Debt (market value) (£)	2,000,000	0	0	2,000,000	2,000,000
S&P debt rating	A+	n.a.	n.a.	A–	A
Weighted average cost of capital	–	10%	10%	–	–

Based on conversations with management of the five companies, as well as on her own independent research and analysis, White notes the following:

Aquarius:

- Has lower bonding costs than does Bema.
- Has a higher percentage of tangible assets to total assets than does Bema.
- Has a higher degree of operating leverage than does Bema.

Garth:

- Invests significantly less in Research and Development than does Holte.
- Has a more highly developed corporate governance system than does Holte.
- Has more business risk than does Holte.

In addition, White has reached various conclusions regarding announcements by Bema, Garth, and Vega:

Announcement:	Bema has announced that it will issue debt and use the proceeds to repurchase shares. As a result of this debt-financed share repurchase program, Bema indicates that its debt/equity ratio will increase to 0.6 and its before-tax cost of debt will be 6 percent.
Conclusion:	As result of the announced program, Bema's total market value should decrease relative to Aquarius's.

---

[1]Item set developed by Sean Cleary, CFA (Ontario, Canada).

Announcement: Garth has announced that it plans to abandon the prior policy of all-equity financing by the issuance of £1 million in debt in order to buy back an equivalent amount of equity. Garth's before-tax cost of debt is 6 percent.

Conclusion: This change in capital structure is reasonable, but Garth should take care subsequently to maintain a lower D/E ratio than Holte.

Announcement: Vega has announced that it intends to raise capital next year, but is unsure of the appropriate method of raising capital.

Conclusion: White has concluded that Vega should apply the pecking order theory to determine the appropriate method of raising capital.

14. Based on the Modigliani and Miller (MM) propositions with corporate taxes, Aquarius's WACC is *closest* to:
    A. 3.38%.
    B. 7.87%.
    C. 11.25%.

15. Based on MM propositions with corporate taxes, what is Bema's weighted average cost of capital after the completion of their announced debt-financed share repurchase program?
    A. 6.52%.
    B. 7.83%.
    C. 8.88%.

16. Based on Exhibit C and White's notes, which of the following is *least* consistent with White's conclusion regarding Bema's announcement?
    A. Bema's bonding costs will be higher than Aquarius's.
    B. Bema will have a lower degree of operating leverage than does Aquarius.
    C. Bema will have a lower percentage of tangible assets to total assets than does Aquarius.

17. Based on the MM propositions with corporate taxes, Garth's cost of equity after the debt issuance is *closest* to:
    A. 10.00%.
    B. 10.85%.
    C. 11.33%.

18. Based on Exhibit C and White's notes, which of the following is *most* consistent with White's conclusion regarding Garth's announcement?
    A. Garth has more business risk than does Holte.
    B. Garth invests significantly less in Research and Development than does Holte.
    C. Garth has a more highly developed corporate governance system than does Holte.

19. Based on White's conclusion regarding determining the appropriate method of raising capital, Vega should raise capital in the following order:
    A. debt, internal financing, equity.
    B. equity, debt, internal financing.
    C. internal financing, debt, equity.

CHAPTER 6

DIVIDENDS AND SHARE REPURCHASES: BASICS

LEARNING OUTCOMES

After completing this chapter, you will be able to do the following:

- Describe regular cash dividends, extra dividends, stock dividends, stock splits, and reverse stock splits, including their expected effect on a shareholder's wealth and a company's financial ratios.
- Describe dividend payment chronology, including the significance of declaration, holder-of-record, ex-dividend, and payment dates.
- Compare share repurchase methods.
- Calculate and compare the effects of a share repurchase on earnings per share when (1) the repurchase is financed with the company's excess cash and (2) the company uses funded debt to finance the repurchase.
- Calculate the effect of a share repurchase on book value per share.
- Explain why a cash dividend and a share repurchase of the same amount are equivalent in terms of the effect on shareholders' wealth, all else being equal.

SUMMARY OVERVIEW

- Dividends can take the form of regular or irregular cash payments, stock dividends, or stock splits. Only cash dividends are payments to shareholders. Stock dividends and splits merely carve equity into smaller pieces and do not create wealth for shareholders. Reverse stock splits usually occur after a stock has dropped to a very low price and do not affect shareholder wealth—they represent cosmetic repackaging of shareholder equity.
- Regular cash dividends—unlike irregular cash dividends, stock splits, and stock dividends—represent a commitment to pay cash to stockholders on a quarterly, semiannual, or annual basis.
- The key dates for cash dividends, stock dividends, and stock splits are the declaration date, the ex-date, the shareholder-of-record date, and the payment date. Share price will reflect the amount of the cash payment (or shares in the case of a stock dividend or split) on the ex-date.
- Share repurchases, or buybacks, most often occur in the open market. Alternatively, tender offers occur at a fixed price or at a price range through a Dutch auction. Shareholders who do not tender increase their relative position in the company. Direct negotiations with

major shareholders to get them out of the company are less common because they could destroy value for remaining stockholders.

- Share repurchases made with excess cash have the potential to increase earnings per share, whereas share repurchases made with borrowed funds can increase, decrease, or not affect earnings per share, depending on the after-tax borrowing rate.

- A share repurchase is equivalent to the payment of a cash dividend of equal amount in its effect on shareholders' wealth, all other things being equal.

- If the buyback market price is greater (less) than the book value, the book value will decline (increase).

- Announcement of a share repurchase is sometimes accompanied by positive excess returns in the market when the market price is viewed as reflecting management's view that the stock is undervalued, and earnings per share can increase as a result of fewer shares outstanding.

- Initiation of regular cash dividends can also have a positive impact on share value. Management is seen as having enough confidence in the future to make a commitment to pay out cash to shareholders. In addition, some institutional, as well as individual, shareholders see regular cash dividend payments as a measure of investment quality.

PROBLEMS

1. The payment of a 10% stock dividend by a company will result in an increase in that company's:
   A. current ratio.
   B. financial leverage.
   C. contributed capital.

2. If a company's common shares trade at relatively very low prices, that company would be *most likely* to consider the use of a:
   A. stock split.
   B. stock dividend.
   C. reverse stock split.

3. In a recent presentation, Doug Pearce made two statements about dividends:
   Statement 1: "A stock dividend will increase share price, all other things being equal."
   Statement 2: "One practical concern with a stock split is that it will reduce the company's price-to-earnings ratio."
   Are Pearce's two statements about the effects of the stock dividend and stock split correct?
   A. No for both statements.
   B. Yes for Statement 1 and No for Statement 2.
   C. No for Statement 1 and Yes for Statement 2.

4. All other things being equal, the payment of an internally financed cash dividend is *most likely* to result in:
   A. a lower current ratio.
   B. a higher current ratio.
   C. the same current ratio.

5. The calendar dates in Column 1 are potentially significant dates in a typical dividend chronology. Column 2 lists descriptions of these potentially significant dates (in random order).

Column 1	Column 2
Friday, 10 June	A. Holder-of-record date
Thursday, 23 June	B. Declaration date
Friday, 24 June	C. Payment date
Tuesday, 28 June	D. Ex-dividend date
Sunday, 10 July	E. Last day shares trade with the right to receive the dividend

Match the significance of these typical dividend chronology dates by placing the correct letter of the description by the appropriate date. Use the template for your answer.

Dividend Chronology
Friday, 10 June
Thursday, 23 June
Friday, 24 June
Tuesday, 28 June
Sunday, 10 July

6. Mary Young intends to take a position in Megasoft Industries once Megasoft begins paying dividends. A dividend of C$4 is payable by Megasoft on 2 December. The ex-dividend date for the dividend is 10 November, and the holder-of-record date is 12 November. What is the last possible date for Young to purchase her shares if she wants to receive the dividend?
   A. 9 November.
   B. 10 November.
   C. 12 November.

7. Aiken Instruments (AIK) has recently declared a regular quarterly dividend of $0.50, payable on 12 November, with an ex-dividend date of 28 October. Which date below would be the holder-of-record date assuming all the days listed are business days and that trades settle three business days after the trade date?
   A. 27 October.
   B. 30 October.
   C. 11 November.

8. A company has 1 million shares outstanding and earnings are £2 million. The company decides to use £10 million in idle cash to repurchase shares in the open market. The

company's shares are trading at £50 per share. If the company uses the entire £10 million of idle cash to repurchase shares at the market price, the company's earnings per share will be *closest* to:

A. £2.00.

B. £2.30.

C. £2.50.

9. Devon Ltd. common shares sell at $40 a share and their estimated price-to-earnings ratio (P/E) is 32. If Devon borrows funds to repurchase shares at its after-tax cost of debt of 5%, its EPS is *most likely* to:

A. increase.

B. decrease.

C. remain the same.

10. A company can borrow funds at an after-tax cost of 4.5%. The company's stock price is $40 per share, earnings per share is $2.00, and the company has 15 million shares outstanding. If the company borrows just enough to repurchase 2 million shares of stock at the prevailing market price, that company's earnings per share is *most likely* to:

A. increase.

B. decrease.

C. remain the same.

11. Crozet Corporation plans to borrow just enough money to repurchase 100,000 shares. The following information relates to the share repurchase:

Shares outstanding before buyback	3.1 million
Earnings per share before buyback	$4.00
Share price at time of buyback	$50
After-tax cost of borrowing	6%

Crozet's earnings per share after the buyback will be *closest* to:

A. $4.03.

B. $4.10.

C. $4.23.

12. A company with 20 million shares outstanding decides to repurchase 2 million shares at the prevailing market price of €30 per share. At the time of the buyback, the company reports total assets of €850 million and total liabilities of €250 million. As a result of the buyback, that company's book value per share will *most likely*:

A. increase.

B. decrease.

C. remain the same.

13. An analyst gathered the following information about a company:

Number of shares outstanding	10 million
Earnings per share	$2.00
P/E	20
Book value per share	$30

    If the company repurchases 1 million shares at the prevailing market price, the resulting book value per share will be *closest* to:
    A. $26.
    B. $27.
    C. $29.

14. If a company's objective is to support its stock price in the event of a market downturn, it would be advised to authorize:
    A. a Dutch auction tender offer effective in 30 days.
    B. a tender offer share repurchase at a fixed price effective in 30 days.
    C. an open market share repurchase plan to be executed over the next five years.

15. A company has positive free cash flow and is considering whether to use the entire amount of that free cash flow to pay a special cash dividend or to repurchase shares at the prevailing market price. Shareholders' wealth under the two options will be equivalent unless the:
    A. company's book value per share is less than the prevailing market price.
    B. company's book value per share is greater than the prevailing market price.
    C. tax consequences and/or information content for each alternative is different.

16. Assume that a company is based in a country that has no taxes on dividends or capital gains. The company is considering either paying a special dividend or repurchasing its own shares. Shareholders of the company would have:
    A. greater wealth if the company repurchased its shares.
    B. greater wealth if the company paid a special cash dividend.
    C. the same wealth under either a cash dividend or share repurchase program.

CHAPTER 7

DIVIDENDS AND SHARE REPURCHASES: ANALYSIS

LEARNING OUTCOMES

After completing this chapter, you will be able to do the following:

- Compare theories of dividend policy and explain implications of each for share value, given a description of a corporate dividend action.
- Describe types of information (signals) that dividend initiations, increases, decreases, and omissions may convey.
- Explain how clientele effects and agency issues may affect a company's payout policy.
- Explain factors that affect dividend policy.
- Calculate and interpret the effective tax rate on a given currency unit of corporate earnings under double-taxation, split-rate, and tax imputation dividend tax regimes.
- Compare stable dividend, target payout, and residual dividend policies and calculate the dividend under each policy.
- Explain the choice between paying cash dividends and repurchasing shares.
- Describe global trends in corporate dividend policies.
- Calculate and interpret dividend coverage ratios based on (1) net income and (2) free cash flow.
- Identify characteristics of companies that may not be able to sustain their cash dividend.

SUMMARY OVERVIEW

- There are three general theories on investor preference for dividends. The first, MM, argues that given perfect markets dividend policy is irrelevant. The "bird in hand" theory contends that investors value a dollar of dividends today more than uncertain capital gains in the future. The third theory argues that in countries in which dividends are taxed at higher rates than capital gains, taxable investors should prefer that companies reinvest earnings in growth opportunities or repurchase shares so they receive more of the return in the form of capital gains.
- An argument for dividend irrelevance given perfect markets is that the corporate dividend policy is irrelevant because shareholders can create their preferred cash flow stream by selling any company's shares ("homemade dividends").

- The clientele effect suggests that different classes of investors have differing preferences for dividend income. Those who prefer dividends will tend to invest in higher yielding shares.
- Dividend declarations may provide information to current and prospective shareholders regarding the prospects of the company. Initiating a dividend or increasing a dividend sends a positive signal, whereas cutting a dividend or omitting a dividend typically sends a negative signal.
- Payment of dividends can help reduce the agency conflicts between managers and shareholders, but can worsen conflicts of interest between shareholders and debt holders.
- Empirically, several factors appear to influence dividend policy, including investment opportunities for the company, the volatility expected in its future earnings, financial flexibility, tax considerations, flotation costs, and contractual and legal restrictions.
- Under double taxation systems, dividends are taxed at both the corporate and shareholder level. Under tax imputation systems, a shareholder receives a credit on dividends for the tax paid on corporate profits. Under split-rate taxation systems, corporate profits are taxed at different rates depending on whether the profits are retained or paid out in dividends.
- Companies with outstanding debt often are restricted in the amount of dividends they can pay because of debt covenants and legal restrictions. Some institutions require that a company pay a dividend to be on their "approved" list. If a company funds capital expenditures by borrowing while paying earnings out in dividends, it will incur flotation costs on new issues.
- Using a stable dividend policy, a company tries to align its dividend growth rate to the company's long-term earnings growth rate. Dividends may increase even in years when earnings decline, and dividends will increase at a lower rate than earnings in boom years.
- According to Lintner (1956), the stable dividend policy can be represented by a gradual adjustment process in which the expected dividend is equal to last year's dividend per share, plus [(this year's expected increase in earnings per share) × (the target payout ratio) × (an annual adjustment factor)].
- Using a constant dividend payout ratio policy, a company applies a target dividend payout ratio to current earnings; therefore, dividends are more volatile than with a stable dividend policy.
- In a residual dividend policy, the amount of the annual dividend is equal to annual earnings minus the capital budget times the percent of the capital budget to be financed through retained earnings or zero, whichever is greater. An advantage of this policy is that positive NPV opportunities have the first priority in the use of earnings.
- Companies can repurchase shares in lieu of increasing cash dividends. Share repurchases usually offer more flexibility than cash dividends by not establishing the expectation that a particular level of cash distribution will be maintained.
- Companies can pay regular cash dividends supplemented by share repurchases. In years of extraordinary increases in earnings, share repurchases can substitute for special cash dividends.
- Share repurchases can signal that company officials think their shares are undervalued. On the other hand, share repurchases could send a negative signal that the company has few positive NPV opportunities.
- The issue of dividend safety deals with how safe a company's dividend actually is, specifically whether the company's earnings and, more importantly, its cash flow are sufficient to sustain the payment of the dividend.
- Early warning signs of whether a company can sustain its dividend include the level of dividend yield, whether the company borrows to pay the dividend, and the company's past dividend record.

PROBLEMS

1. Match the phrases in Column A with the corresponding dividend theory in Column B. Note that you may use the answers in Column B more than once.

Column A	Column B
1. Bird in the hand	a) dividend policy matters
2. Homemade dividends	b) dividend policy is irrelevant
3. High tax rates on dividends	

2. Which of the following assumptions is *not* required for Miller and Modigliani's (MM) dividend theory?
   A. There are no taxes.
   B. Investors sort themselves into dividend clienteles.
   C. Shareholders have no transaction costs when buying and selling shares.

3. The clientele effect implies that:
   A. investors prefer high dividend paying shares.
   B. investors have varying preferences regarding dividends.
   C. low tax bracket investors are indifferent to dividends.

4. Sophie Chan owns 100,000 shares of PAT Company. PAT is selling for €40 per share, so her investment is worth €4,000,000. Chan reinvests the gross amount of all dividends received to purchase additional shares. Assume that the clientele for PAT shares consists of tax-exempt investors. If PAT pays a €1.50 dividend, Chan's new share ownership after reinvesting dividends at the ex-dividend price would be *closest* to:
   A. 103,600.
   B. 103,750.
   C. 103,900.

5. Which of the following is *most likely* to signal negative information concerning a company?
   A. Share repurchase.
   B. Decrease in the quarterly dividend rate.
   C. A two-for-one stock split.

6. WL Corporation is located in a jurisdiction that has a 40% corporate tax rate on pretax income and a 30% personal tax rate on dividends. WL distributes all its after-tax income to shareholders. What is the effective tax rate on WL pretax income distributed in dividends?
   A. 42%.
   B. 58%.
   C. 70%.

7. Which of the following factors would *not* tend to be associated with a company having a low dividend payout ratio?
   A. Low growth prospects.
   B. High tax rates on dividends.
   C. High flotation costs on new equity issues.

8. The dividend policy of Berkshire Gardens Inc. can be represented by a gradual adjustment to a target dividend payout ratio. Last year Berkshire had earnings per share of $3.00 and paid a dividend of $0.60 a share. This year it estimates earnings per share will be $4.00. Find its dividend per share for this year if it has a 25% target payout ratio and uses a five-year period to adjust its dividend.
   A. $0.65.
   B. $0.80.
   C. $0.85.

9. The Apex Corp. has a target debt/equity ratio of 40/60. Its capital budget for next year is estimated to be $40 million. Estimated net income is $30 million. If Apex follows a residual dividend policy, its dividend is expected to be:
   A. $6 million.
   B. $12 million.
   C. $18 million.

10. Beta Corporation is a manufacturer of inflatable furniture. Which of the following scenarios *best* reflects a stable dividend policy for Beta?
    A. Maintaining a constant dividend payout ratio of 40–50%.
    B. Maintaining the dividend at $1.00 a share for several years given no change in Beta's long-term prospects.
    C. Increasing the dividend 5% a year over several years to reflect the two years in which Beta recognized mark-to-market gains on derivative positions.

11. Investors may prefer companies that repurchase their shares instead of paying a cash dividend when:
    A. capital gains are taxed at lower rates than dividends.
    B. capital gains are taxed at the same rate as dividends.
    C. the company needs more equity to finance capital expenditures.

The following information relates to Questions 12–14.
   Janet Wu is treasurer of Wilson Paper Company, a manufacturer of paper products for the office and school markets. Wilson Paper is selling one of its divisions for $70 million cash. Wu is considering whether to recommend a special dividend of $70 million or a repurchase of 2 million shares of Wilson common stock in the open market. She is reviewing some possible effects of the buyback with the company's financial analyst. Wilson has a long-term record of gradually increasing earnings and dividends. Wilson's board has also approved capital spending of $15 million to be entirely funded out of this year's earnings.

Book value of equity	$750 million ($30 a share)
Shares outstanding	25 million
12-month trading range	$25–$35
Current share price	$35
After-tax cost of borrowing	7%

Estimated full year earnings	$25 million
Last year's dividends	$9 million
Target debt/equity (market value)	35/65

12. In investors' minds, Wilson's share buyback could be a signal that the company:
    A. is decreasing its financial leverage.
    B. views its shares as undervalued in the marketplace.
    C. has more investment opportunities than it could fund internally.

13. Assume that Wilson Paper funds its capital spending out of its estimated full year earnings. If Wilson uses a residual dividend policy, determine Wilson's implied dividend payout ratio.
    A. 36%.
    B. 40%.
    C. 60%.

14. The *most likely* tax environment in which Wilson Paper's shareholders would prefer that Wilson repurchase its shares (share buybacks) instead of paying dividends is one in which:
    A. the tax rate on capital gains and dividends is the same.
    B. capital gains tax rates are higher than dividend income tax rates.
    C. capital gains tax rates are lower than dividend income tax rates.

CHAPTER 8

WORKING CAPITAL MANAGEMENT

LEARNING OUTCOMES

After completing this chapter, you will be able to do the following:

- Describe primary sources of liquidity and factors that influence a company's liquidity position.
- Compare a company's liquidity measures with those of peer companies.
- Evaluate working capital effectiveness of a company based on its operating and cash conversion cycles, and compare the company's effectiveness with that of peer companies.
- Explain the effect of different types of cash flows on a company's net daily cash position.
- Identify and evaluate the necessary tools to use in managing a company's net daily cash position.
- Calculate and interpret comparable yields on various securities, compare portfolio returns against a standard benchmark, and evaluate a company's short-term investment policy guidelines.
- Evaluate a company's management of accounts receivable, inventory, and accounts payable over time and compared to peer companies.
- Evaluate the choices of short-term funding available to a company and recommend a financing method.

SUMMARY OVERVIEW

- Understanding how to evaluate a company's liquidity position.
- Calculating and interpreting operating and cash conversion cycles.
- Evaluating overall working capital effectiveness of a company and comparing it with other peer companies.
- Identifying the components of a cash forecast to be able to prepare a short-term (i.e., up to one year) cash forecast.
- Understanding the common types of short-term investments, and computing comparable yields on securities.
- Measuring the performance of a company's accounts receivable function.
- Measuring the financial performance of a company's inventory management function.
- Measuring the performance of a company's accounts payable function.
- Evaluating the short-term financing choices available to a company and recommending a financing method.

63

PROBLEMS

1. Suppose a company has a current ratio of 2.5 times and a quick ratio of 1.5 times. If the company's current liabilities are €100 million, the amount of inventory is *closest* to:
   A. €50 million.
   B. €100 million.
   C. €150 million.

2. Given the following financial statement data, calculate the operating cycle for this company.

	In millions
Credit sales	$25,000
Cost of goods sold	$20,000
Accounts receivable	$2,500
Inventory – Beginning balance	$2,000
Inventory – Ending balance	$2,300
Accounts payable	$1,700

   The operating cycle for this company is *closest* to:
   A. 42.0 days.
   B. 47.9 days.
   C. 78.5 days.

3. Given the following financial statement data, calculate the net operating cycle for this company.

	In millions
Credit sales	$40,000
Cost of goods sold	$30,000
Accounts receivable	$3,000
Inventory – Beginning balance	$1,500
Inventory – Ending balance	$2,000
Accounts payable	$4,000

   The net operating cycle of this company is *closest* to:
   A. 3.8 days.
   B. 24.3 days.
   C. 51.7 days.

4. The bond equivalent yield for a 182-day U.S. Treasury bill that has a price of $9,725 per $10,000 face value is *closest* to:
   A. 5.44%.
   B. 5.53%.
   C. 5.67%.

5. A company increasing its credit terms for customers from 1/10, net 30 to 1/10, net 60 will *most likely* experience:
   A. an increase in cash on hand.
   B. a higher level of uncollectible accounts.
   C. an increase in the average collection period.

6. Suppose a company uses trade credit with the terms of 2/10, net 50. If the company pays their account on the 50th day, the effective borrowing cost of skipping the discount on day 10 is *closest* to:
   A. 14.9%.
   B. 15.0%.
   C. 20.2%.

7. William Jones is evaluating three possible means of borrowing $1 million for one month:
   • Drawing down on a line of credit at 7.2% with a ½% commitment fee on the full amount with no compensating balances.
   • A banker's acceptance at 7.1%, an all-inclusive rate.
   • Commercial paper at 6.9% with a dealer's commission of ¼% and a backup line cost of ⅓%, both of these would be assessed on the $1 million of commercial paper issued.
   Which of these forms of borrowing results in the lowest cost of credit?
   A. Line of credit.
   B. Banker's acceptance.
   C. Commercial paper.

The following information relates to Questions 8–12.
Mary Gonzales is evaluating companies in the office supply industry and has compiled the following information:

Company	20X1 Credit Sales ($)	20X1 Average Receivables Balance ($)	20X2 Credit Sales ($)	20X2 Average Receivables Balance ($)
A	5.0 million	1.0 million	6.0 million	1.2 million
B	3.0 million	1.2 million	4.0 million	1.5 million
C	2.5 million	0.8 million	3.0 million	1.0 million
D	0.5 million	0.1 million	0.6 million	0.2 million
Industry	25.0 million	5.0 million	28.0 million	5.4 million

8. Which company had the highest number of days of receivables for the year 20X1?
   A. Company A.
   B. Company B.
   C. Company C.

9. Which company has the lowest accounts receivable turnover in the year 20X2?
   A. Company A.
   B. Company B.
   C. Company D.

10. The industry average receivables collection period:
    A. increased from 20X1 to 20X2.
    B. decreased from 20X1 to 20X2.
    C. did not change from 20X1 to 20X2.

11. Which company reduced the average time it took to collect on accounts receivable from 20X1 to 20X2?
    A. Company B.
    B. Company C.
    C. Company D.

12. Gonzales determined that Company A had an operating cycle of 100 days in 20X2, whereas Company D had an operating cycle of 145 days for the same fiscal year. This means that:
    A. Company D's inventory turnover is less than that of Company A.
    B. Company D's inventory turnover is greater than that of Company A.
    C. Company D's cash conversion cycle is shorter than that of Company A.

CHAPTER 9

FINANCIAL STATEMENT ANALYSIS

LEARNING OUTCOMES

After completing this chapter, you will be able to do the following:

- Interpret common-size balance sheets and common-size income statements and demonstrate their use by applying either vertical analysis or horizontal analysis.
- Calculate and interpret measures of a company's operating efficiency, internal liquidity (liquidity ratios), solvency, and profitability, and demonstrate the use of these measures in company analysis.
- Calculate and interpret variations of the DuPont expression and demonstrate use of the DuPont approach in corporate analysis.
- Calculate and interpret basic earnings per share and diluted earnings per share.
- Calculate and interpret book value of equity per share, price-to-earnings ratio, dividends per share, dividend payout ratio, and plowback ratio.
- Demonstrate the use of pro forma income and balance sheet statements.

SUMMARY OVERVIEW

A challenge that we face in financial analysis is making sense of the wealth of information that is available about a company and the industry in which it operates. Companies provide shareholders and investors with quarterly and annual financial statements, as well as numerous other financial releases. Financial ratio analysis and common-size analysis help us gauge the financial performance and condition of a company through an examination of relationships among these many financial items.

A thorough financial analysis of a company requires examining its efficiency in putting its assets to work, its liquidity position, its solvency, and its profitability. We can use the tools of common-size analysis and financial ratio analysis, including the DuPont model, to help understand where a company has been. We then apply these relationships in pro forma analysis, forecasting the company's income statements and balance sheets for future periods, to see how the company's performance is likely to evolve.

PROBLEMS

The following information relates to Problems 1, 2, and 3.

Tab, Inc., Income Statements for Fiscal Years 2003, 2004, and 2005

| | Amount (in millions of dollars) | | |
	2005	2004	2003
Revenues	$25,000	$22,000	$21,000
Cost of sales	20,000	18,000	17,000
Gross profit	$5,000	$4,000	$4,000
Selling, general, and administrative expenses	500	500	800
Operating income	$4,500	$3,500	$3,200
Interest and other nonoperating expense	200	250	250
Earnings before income taxes	$4,300	$3,250	$2,950
Income tax	1,410	975	885
Net income	$2,890	$2,275	$2,065

Tab, Inc., Balance Sheets as of End of Fiscal Years 2003, 2004, and 2005

| | Amount (in millions of dollars) | | |
	2005	2004	2003
Cash, cash equiv., and marketable securities	$200	$150	$100
Accounts receivable	1,800	1,350	900
Inventories	8,000	7,500	7,000
Total current assets	$10,000	$9,000	$8,000
Net property, plant, and equipment	$20,000	19,000	19,000
Intangible assets	1,000	1,000	1,000
Total assets	$31,000	$29,000	$28,000
Accounts payable	$500	$790	$615
Debt due in one year	1,000	1,000	1,000
Long-term debt	12,000	13,000	14,000
Shareholders' equity	17,500	14,210	12,385
Total liabilities and equity	$31,000	$29,000	$28,000

1. Using vertical common-size analysis and restating the balance sheets using total assets as the benchmark to analyze changes at Tab between fiscal year 2003 and fiscal year 2005, an analyst would correctly conclude that Tab:
   A. reduced its relative investment in inventory.
   B. increased the role of intangible assets in its investments.
   C. decreased its reliance on debt financing relative to equity financing.

2. Using vertical common-size analysis of the income statement of Tab for 2005, the cost of sales relative to the benchmark is *closest* to:
   A. 75%.
   B. 80%.
   C. 85%.

3. Using horizontal common-size analysis of the income statement of Tab for 2005, the cost of sales relative to the benchmark of 2003 is *closest* to:
   A. 95%.
   B. 118%.
   C. 123%.

4. Common-size analysis is used in financial analysis to:
   A. evaluate changes in a company's operating cycle over time.
   B. compare companies of different sizes or to compare a company with itself over time.
   C. restate each element in a company's financial statement as a proportion of the similar account for another company in the same industry.

5. The TBI Company has a number of days of inventory of 50. Therefore, the TBI Company's inventory turnover is *closest* to:
   A. 4.8 times.
   B. 7.3 times.
   C. 8.4 times.

6. The difference between a company's operating cycle and its net operating cycle is:
   A. the number of days that it takes, on average, for the company to sell its inventory.
   B. the number of days that it takes the company to pay on the accounts due its suppliers.
   C. the number of days that it takes for the company's cash investment in inventory to result in cash collections from customers.

7. The net operating cycle is:
   A. inversely related to a company's need for liquidity.
   B. the length of time it takes for an investment in inventory to be returned from collected accounts.
   C. the sum of the number of days of inventory and the number of days of receivables, less the number of days of payables.

8. A measure of the extent to which a company is able to satisfy its short-term obligations is referred to as:
   A. a liquidity ratio.
   B. an activity ratio.
   C. a financial leverage ratio.

9. Which of the following *best* describes the relationship between the current ratio and the cash ratio?
   A. The current ratio and the cash ratio should not bear any relation to one another.
   B. The current ratio is at least equal to the cash ratio but may be larger than the cash ratio.
   C. The cash ratio is at least equal to the current ratio but may be larger than the current ratio.

10. Suppose a company has earnings before taxes of $20 billion and its income tax is 35% of its earnings before taxes. If the company has an interest expense of $2 billion, its interest coverage ratio is *closest* to:
    A. 6.5 times.
    B. 10.0 times.
    C. 11.0 times.

11. If a company has a net profit margin of 12% and a tax rate of 40%, the before-tax profit margin is *closest* to:
    A. 7.2%.
    B. 12.4%.
    C. 20.0%.

12. If a company's operating profit margin is 4% and its total asset turnover is 1.5 times, its operating return on assets is:
    A. 2.7%.
    B. 6.0%.
    C. 7.3%.

13. DuPont analysis involves breaking return-on-assets ratios into their:
    A. marginal and average components.
    B. operating and financing components.
    C. profit margin and turnover components.

14. The DuPont system allows us to break down the return on equity into:
    A. return on assets and the financial leverage ratio.
    B. profit margin, the tax retention ratio, and inventory turnover.
    C. gross profit margin, total asset turnover, and the debt-to-equity ratio.

15. If a company's net profit margin is –5%, its total asset turnover is 1.5 times, and its financial leverage ratio is 1.2 times, its return on equity is *closest* to:
    A. –9.0%.
    B. –7.5%.
    C. –3.2%.

The following information relates to Problems 16 and 17.

LaPearla Company Income Statement for Year 2005 (in millions)		LaPearla Company Balance Sheet, End of Year 2005 (in millions)	
Revenues	€10,000	Current assets	€2,000
Cost of goods sold	5,500	Net plant and equipment	18,000
Gross profit	€4,500	Total assets	€20,000
Selling, general, and administrative expenses	800		
Operating income	€3,700	Current liabilities	€1,000
Interest expense	500	Long-term debt	5,000
Earnings before taxes	€3,200	Common stock and paid-in capital	500
Taxes	960	Retained earnings	13,500
Net income	€2,240	Total liabilities and equity	€20,000

16. Suppose that LaPearla's revenues are expected to grow at a rate of 10% and all elements of the income statement and balance sheet are sales-driven except for the tax burden, which remains at 30%. LaPearla's pro forma net income for 2006 is *closest* to:
    A. €2.2 billion.
    B. €2.5 billion.
    C. €2.8 billion.

17. If LaPearla's long-term debt and paid-in capital accounts remain at their 2005 levels, the tax rate remains at the 2005 rate, and all other income statement and balance sheet accounts are sales-driven with an expected growth rate of revenues of 10%, in 2006 LaPearla will have a financing:
    A. deficiency if it pays no dividends.
    B. surplus if it pays out 50% of its net income in dividends.
    C. deficiency if it pays out 50% of its net income in dividends.

CHAPTER 10

MERGERS AND ACQUISITIONS

LEARNING OUTCOMES

After completing this chapter, you will be able to do the following:

- Classify merger and acquisition (M&A) activities based on forms of integration and types of mergers.
- Explain common motivations behind M&A activity.
- Explain how earnings per share (EPS) bootstrapping works and calculate a company's post-merger EPS.
- Explain the relationship among merger motivations and types of mergers based on industry life cycles.
- Contrast merger transaction characteristics by form of acquisition, method of payment, and attitude of target management.
- Distinguish among pre-offer and post-offer takeover defense mechanisms.
- Calculate the Herfindahl–Hirschman Index (HHI) and evaluate the likelihood of an antitrust challenge for a given business combination.
- Compare the discounted cash flow, comparable company, and comparable transaction analyses for valuing a target company, including the advantages and disadvantages of each.
- Calculate free cash flows for a target company and estimate the company's intrinsic value based on discounted cash flow analysis.
- Estimate the value of a target company using comparable company and comparable transaction analyses.
- Evaluate a merger bid, calculate the estimated post-merger value of an acquirer, and calculate the gains accrued to the target shareholders versus the acquirer shareholders.
- Explain the effects of price and payment method on the distribution of risks and benefits in a merger transaction.
- Describe empirical evidence related to the distribution of benefits in a merger.
- Distinguish among divestitures, equity carve-outs, spin-offs, split-offs, and liquidation.
- Explain major reasons for divestitures.

SUMMARY OVERVIEW

- An acquisition is the purchase of some portion of one company by another. A merger represents the absorption of one company by another such that only one entity survives following the transaction.

- Mergers can be categorized by the form of integration. In a statutory merger, one company is merged into another; in a subsidiary merger, the target becomes a subsidiary of the acquirer; and in a consolidation, both the acquirer and target become part of a newly formed company.

- Horizontal mergers occur among peer companies engaged in the same kind of business. Vertical mergers occur among companies along a given value chain. Conglomerates are formed by companies in unrelated businesses.

- Merger activity has historically occurred in waves. These waves have typically coincided with a strong economy and buoyant stock market activity. Merger activity tends to be concentrated in a few industries, usually those undergoing changes, such as deregulation or technological advancement.

- The motives for M&A activity include synergy, growth, market power, the acquisition of unique capabilities and resources, diversification, increased earnings, management's personal incentives, tax considerations, and the possibilities of uncovering hidden value. Cross-border motivations may involve technology transfer, product differentiation, government policy, and the opportunities to serve existing clients abroad.

- A merger transaction may take the form of a stock purchase (when the acquirer gives the target company's shareholders some combination of cash or securities in exchange for shares of the target company's stock) or an asset purchase (when the acquirer purchases the target company's assets and payment is made directly to the target company). The decision of which approach to take will affect other aspects of the transaction, such as how approval is obtained, which laws apply, how the liabilities are treated, and how the shareholders and the company are taxed.

- The method of payment for a merger can be cash, securities, or a mixed offering with some of both. The exchange ratio in a stock or mixed offering determines the number of shares that stockholders in the target company will receive in exchange for each of their shares in the target company.

- Hostile transactions are those opposed by target managers, whereas friendly transactions are endorsed by the target company's managers. There are a variety of both pre- and post-offer defenses a target can use to ward off an unwanted takeover bid.

- Examples of pre-offer defense mechanisms include poison pills and puts, incorporation in a jurisdiction with restrictive takeover laws, staggered boards of directors, restricted voting rights, supermajority voting provisions, fair price amendments, and golden parachutes.

- Examples of post-offer defenses include "just say no" defense, litigation, greenmail, share repurchases, leveraged recapitalization, "crown jewel" defense, "Pac-Man" defense, or finding a white knight or a white squire.

- Antitrust legislation prohibits mergers and acquisitions that impede competition. Major U.S. antitrust legislation includes the Sherman Antitrust Act, the Clayton Act, the Celler–Kefauver Act, and the Hart–Scott–Rodino Act.

- The Federal Trade Commission and Department of Justice review mergers for antitrust concerns in the United States. The European Commission reviews transactions in the European Union.

- The Herfindahl–Hirschman Index (HHI) is a measure of market power based on the sum of the squared market shares for each company in an industry. Higher index values or combinations that result in a large jump in the index are more likely to meet regulatory challenges.

- The Williams Act is the cornerstone of securities legislation for M&A activities in the United States. The Williams Act ensures a fair tender offer process through the establishment of disclosure requirements and formal tender offer procedures.

- Three major tools for valuing a target company are discounted cash flow analysis (which involves discounting free cash flows estimated with pro forma financial statements), comparable company analysis (which estimates a company's intrinsic value based on relative valuation metrics for similar companies), and comparable transaction analysis (which derives valuation from details of recent takeover transactions for comparable companies).

- In a merger bid, the gain to target shareholders is measured as the control premium, which equals the price paid for the target company in excess of its value. The acquirer gains equal the value of any synergies created by the merger minus the premium paid to target shareholders. Together, the bid and the method of payment determine the distribution of risks and returns among acquirer and target shareholders with regard to realization of synergies as well as correct estimation of the target company's value.

- The empirical evidence suggests that merger transactions create value for target company shareholders. Acquirers, in contrast, tend to accrue value in the years following a merger. This finding suggests that synergies are often overestimated or difficult to achieve.

- When a company decides to sell, liquidate, or spin off a division or a subsidiary, it is referred to as a divestiture. Companies may divest assets for a variety of reasons, including a change in strategic focus, poor fit of the asset within the corporation, reverse synergy, or cash flow needs.

- The three basic ways that a company divests assets are a sale to another company, a spin-off to shareholders, and liquidation.

PROBLEMS

The following information relates to Questions 1–6.

Modern Auto, an automobile parts supplier, has made an offer to acquire Sky Systems, creator of software for the airline industry. The offer is to pay Sky Systems' shareholders the current market value of their stock in Modern Auto's stock. The relevant information it used in those calculations is given below:

	Modern Auto	Sky Systems
Share price	$40	$25
Number of outstanding shares (millions)	40	15
Earnings (millions)	$100	$30

Although the total earnings of the combined company will not increase and are estimated to be $130 million, Charles Wilhelm (treasurer of Modern Auto) argues that there are two attractive reasons to merge. First, Wilhelm says, "The merger of Modern Auto and Sky Systems will result in lower risk for our shareholders because of the diversification effect." Second, Wilhelm also says, "If our EPS increases, our stock price will increase in line with the EPS increase because our P/E will stay the same."

Sky Systems' managers are not interested in the offer by Modern Auto. The managers, instead, approach HiFly, Inc., which is in the same industry as Sky Systems, to see if it would be interested in acquiring Sky Systems. HiFly is interested, and both companies believe there will be synergies from this acquisition. If HiFly were to acquire Sky Systems, it would do so by paying $400 million in cash.

HiFly is somewhat concerned whether antitrust regulators would consider the acquisition of Sky Systems an antitrust violation. The market in which the two companies operate consists of eight competitors. The largest company has a 25 percent market share. HiFly has the second-largest market share of 20 percent. Five companies, including Sky Systems, each have a market share of 10 percent. The smallest company has a 5 percent market share.

1. The acquisition of Sky Systems by Modern Auto and the acquisition of Sky Systems by HiFly, respectively, would be examples of a:
   A. vertical merger and a horizontal merger.
   B. conglomerate merger and a vertical merger.
   C. conglomerate merger and a horizontal merger.

2. If Sky Systems were to be acquired by Modern Auto under the terms of the original offer, the post-merger EPS of the new company would be *closest* to:
   A. $2.00.
   B. $2.32.
   C. $2.63.

3. Are Wilhelm's two statements about his shareholders benefiting from the diversification effect of the merger and about the increase in the stock price, respectively, correct?

	The Merger Will Result in Lower Risk for Shareholders	Stock Price Will Increase in Line with the EPS Increase
A.	No	No
B.	No	Yes
C.	Yes	No

4. Which of the following defenses *best* describes the role of HiFly in the acquisition scenario?
   A. Crown jewel.
   B. Pac-Man.
   C. White knight.

5. Suppose HiFly acquires Sky Systems for the stated terms. The gain to Sky Systems shareholders resulting from the merger transaction would be *closest* to:
   A. $25 million.
   B. $160 million.
   C. $375 million.

6. If HiFly and Sky Systems attempt to merge, the increase in the Herfindahl–Hirschman Index (HHI) and the probable action by the Department of Justice and the FTC, respectively, in response to the merger announcement are:

	Increase in the HHI	Probable Response of Department of Justice and FTC
A.	290	To challenge the merger
B.	290	To investigate the merger
C.	400	To challenge the merger

The following information relates to Questions 7–12.

Kinetic Corporation is considering acquiring High Tech Systems. Jim Smith, the vice president of finance at Kinetic, has been assigned the task of estimating a fair acquisition price for High Tech. Smith is aware of several approaches that could be used for this purpose. He plans to estimate the acquisition price based on each of these approaches, and has collected or estimated the necessary financial data.

High Tech has 10 million shares of common stock outstanding and no debt. Smith has estimated that the post-merger free cash flows from High Tech, in millions of dollars, would be 15, 17, 20, and 23 at the end of the following four years. After Year 4, he projects the free cash flow to grow at a constant rate of 6.5 percent a year. He determines that the appropriate rate for discounting these estimated cash flows is 11 percent. He also estimates that after four years High Tech would be worth 23 times its free cash flow at the end of the fourth year.

Smith has determined that three companies—Alpha, Neutron, and Techno—are comparable to High Tech. He has also identified three recent takeover transactions—Quadrant, ProTech, and Automator—that are similar to the takeover of High Tech under consideration. He believes that price-to-earnings, price-to-sales, and price-to-book value per share of these companies could be used to estimate the value of High Tech. The relevant data for the three comparable companies and for High Tech are as follows:

Valuation Variables	Alpha	Neutron	Techno	High Tech
Current stock price ($)	44.00	23.00	51.00	31.00
Earnings/share ($)	3.01	1.68	2.52	1.98
Sales/share ($)	20.16	14.22	18.15	17.23
Book value/share ($)	15.16	7.18	11.15	10.02

The relevant data for the three recently acquired companies are given below:

Valuation Variables	Quadrant	ProTech	Automator
Stock price pre-takeover ($)	24.90	43.20	29.00
Acquisition stock price ($)	28.00	52.00	34.50
Earnings/share ($)	1.40	2.10	2.35
Sales/share ($)	10.58	20.41	15.93
Book value/share ($)	8.29	10.14	9.17

While discussing his analysis with a colleague, Smith makes two comments. Smith's first comment is: "If there were a pre-announcement run-up in Quadrant's price because of speculation, the takeover premium should be computed based on the price prior to the run-up." His second comment is: "Because the comparable transaction approach is based on the acquisition price, the takeover premium is implicitly recognized in this approach."

7. What is the present value per share of High Tech stock using the discounted cash flow approach if the terminal value of High Tech is based on using the constant growth model to determine terminal value?
   A. $39.38.
   B. $40.56.
   C. $41.57.

8. What is the value per share of High Tech stock using the discounted cash flow approach if the terminal value of High Tech is based on using the cash flow multiple method to determine terminal value?
   A. $35.22.
   B. $40.56.
   C. $41.57.

9. The average stock price of High Tech for the three relative valuation ratios (if it is traded at the mean of the three valuations) is *closest* to:
   A. $35.21.
   B. $39.38.
   C. $40.56.

10. Taking into account the mean takeover premium on recent comparable takeovers, what would be the estimate of the fair acquisition price of High Tech based on the comparable company approach?
    A. $35.22.
    B. $40.83.
    C. $41.29.

11. The fair acquisition price of High Tech using the comparable transaction approach is *closest* to:
    A. $35.22.
    B. $40.86.
    C. $41.31.

12. Are Smith's two comments about his analysis correct?
    A. Both of his comments are correct.
    B. Both of his comments are incorrect.
    C. His first comment is correct, and his second comment is incorrect.

The following information relates to Questions 13–18 and is based on "Corporate Governance" and "Mergers and Acquisitions."

Mark Zin and Stella Lee are CEO and CFO, respectively, of Moonbase Corporation. They are concerned that Moonbase is undervalued and subject to a hostile takeover bid. To assess the value of their own firm, they are reviewing current financial data for Jupiter PLC, Saturn Corporation, and Voyager Corporation, three firms they believe are comparable to Moonbase.

Relative Valuation Ratio	Jupiter	Saturn	Voyager
P/E	23.00	19.50	21.50
P/B	4.24	5.25	4.91
P/CF	12.60	11.40	13.30

Zin believes Moonbase should trade at similar multiples to these firms and that each valuation ratio measure is equally valid. Moonbase has a current stock price of $34.00 per share, earnings of $1.75 per share, book value of $8.50 per share, and cash flow of $3.20 per share. Using the average of each of the three multiples for the three comparable firms, Zin finds that Moonbase is undervalued.

Lee states that the low valuation reflects current poor performance of a subsidiary of Moonbase. She recommends that the board of directors consider divesting the subsidiary in a manner that would provide cash inflow to Moonbase.

Zin proposes that some action should be taken before a hostile takeover bid is made. He asks Lee if changes can be made to the corporate governance structure in order to make it more difficult for an unwanted suitor to succeed.

In response, Lee makes two comments of actions that would make a hostile takeover more difficult. Lee's first comment is "Moonbase can institute a poison pill that allows our shareholders, other than the hostile bidder, to purchase shares at a substantial discount to current market value." Lee's second comment is: "Moonbase can instead institute a poison put. The put allows shareholders the opportunity to redeem their shares at a substantial premium to current market value."

Zin is also concerned about the general attitude of outside investors with the governance of Moonbase. He has read brokerage reports indicating that the Moonbase governance ratings are generally low. Zin believes the following statements describe characteristics that should provide Moonbase with a strong governance rating.

Statement 1:   Moonbase's directors obtain advice from the corporate counsel to aid them in assessing the firm's compliance with regulatory requirements.

Statement 2:   Five of the ten members of the board of directors are not employed by Moonbase and are considered independent. Though not employed by the company, two of the independent directors are former executives of the company and thus can contribute useful expertise relevant for the business.

Statement 3:   The audit committee of the board is organized so as to have sufficient resources to carry out its task, with an internal staff that reports routinely and directly to the audit committee.

Zin is particularly proud of the fact that Moonbase has begun drafting a "Statement of Corporate Governance" (SCG) that would be available on the company website for viewing by shareholders, investment analysts, and any interested stakeholders. In particular, the SCG pays special attention to policies that ensure effective contributions from the board of directors. These policies include:

Policy #1:   Training is provided to directors prior to joining the board and periodically thereafter.

Policy #2: Statements are provided of management's assessment of the board's performance of its fiduciary responsibilities.

Policy #3: Statements are provided of directors' responsibilities regarding oversight and
monitoring of the firm's risk management and compliance functions.

Zin concludes the discussion by announcing that Johann Steris, a highly regarded
ex-CFO of a major corporation, is under consideration as a member of an expanded board of
directors. Zin states that Steris meets all the requirements as an independent director
including the fact that he will not violate the interlocking directorship requirement. Steris also
will bring experience as a member of the compensation committee of the board of another
firm. He also comments that Steris desires to serve on either the audit or compensation
committee of the Moonbase board and that good governance practice suggests that Steris
would not be prohibited from serving on either committee.

13. The value the CEO estimated based on comparable company analysis is *closest* to:
    A. $37.33.
    B. $39.30.
    C. $40.80.

14. The divestiture technique that Lee is recommending is *most likely*:
    A. a spin-off.
    B. a split-off.
    C. an equity carve-out.

15. With regard to poison pills and puts, Lee's comments are:
    A. correct.
    B. incorrect with regard to the poison put.
    C. incorrect with regard to the poison pill.

16. Which statement by Zin provides the *most* support for a strong governance rating?
    A. Statement 1.
    B. Statement 2.
    C. Statement 3.

17. Which policy of the Statement of Corporate Governance is *least likely* to ensure effective
    contributions from the board of directors?
    A. Policy #1.
    B. Policy #2.
    C. Policy #3.

18. Is Zin's comment that good governance practice does not preclude Steris from serving on
    either of the two committees of the Moonbase board correct?
    A. Yes.
    B. No, good governance practice precludes Steris from serving on the audit committee.
    C. No, good governance practice precludes Steris from serving on the compensation
       committee.

The following information relates to Questions 19–24.
    Josh Logan is a buy-side equity analyst who follows Durtech. Logan's supervisor
believes that Durtech is a likely takeover candidate and has asked Logan to estimate the

company's value per share in the event of an "all stock" takeover bid. Logan plans to estimate Durtech's value per share using three approaches: discounted cash flow, comparable company analysis, and comparable transaction analysis.

Durtech has 1.2 million common shares outstanding and no outstanding long-term debt or preferred stock. Logan estimates that Durtech's free cash flows at the end of the next three years will be $5.0 million, $6.0 million, and $7.0 million, respectively. After Year 3, he projects that free cash flow will grow at five percent per year. He determines the appropriate discount rate for this free cash flow stream is 15 percent per year.

Applying discounted cash flow analysis to the preceding information, Logan determines that Durtech's fair enterprise value is $61.8 million. In a separate analysis based on ratios, Logan estimates that at the end of the third year, Durtech will be worth ten times its year-three free cash flow.

Logan's supervisor is troubled by the sensitivity of his enterprise value calculation to the terminal growth rate assumption. She asks Logan:

"What is the percentage change in your fair enterprise value of $61.8 million if you use a terminal growth rate of zero percent rather than five percent?"

Logan gathers data on two companies comparable to Durtech: Alphatech and Betatech. He believes that price-to-earnings, price-to-sales, and price-to-book-value per share of these companies should be used to value Durtech. The relevant data for the three companies are given in Exhibit A.

EXHIBIT A   Valuation Variables for Durtech and Comparable Companies

Valuation Variables	Alphatech	Betatech	Durtech
Current stock price ($)	72.00	45.00	24.00
Earnings per share ($)	2.00	1.50	1.00
Sales per share ($)	32.00	22.50	16.00
Book value per share ($)	18.00	10.00	8.00

Logan also identifies one recent takeover transaction and analyzes its takeover premium (the amount by which its takeover price per share exceeds its current stock price). Omegatech is comparable to the possible transaction on Durtech. Omegatech had a stock price of $44.40 per share prior to a newspaper report of a takeover rumor. After the takeover rumor was reported, the price rose immediately to $60.30 per share. Eventually, the takeover offer was accepted by Omegatech's shareholders for $55.00 per share. One-year trailing earnings per share for Omegatech immediately prior to the takeover were $1.25 per share.

In order to evaluate the risk of government antitrust action, Logan computes the Herfindahl–Hirschman Index (HHI) for the industry group that includes Durtech. He computes the pre-merger value of the HHI to be 1400. As shown in Exhibit B, Logan also computes the post-merger industry HHI assuming three possible merger scenarios with Durtech.

EXHIBIT B   Post-Merger Industry HHI (assuming merger with Durtech)

Durtech Merger Partner	Post-Merger Industry HHI
Alphatech	1500
Betatech	1510
Gammatech	1520

Based on this analysis, Logan concludes that the industry is moderately concentrated and that a merger of Durtech (with any of the companies listed in Exhibit B) will face a possible government challenge.

19. Using the discounted cash flow approach and assuming that Durtech's terminal value is based on the cash flow multiple method, Logan's best estimate of Durtech's current value per share is *closest* to:
    A. $49.60.
    B. $51.50.
    C. $53.51.

20. Logan's best response to the supervisor's question concerning the sensitivity of the enterprise value to the terminal growth rate assumption is *closest* to:
    A. −36.5%.
    B. −28.5%.
    C. −24.8%.

21. Based on Exhibit A and the mean of each of the valuation ratios, Logan's estimate of Durtech's value per share should be *closest* to:
    A. $30.44.
    B. $33.67.
    C. $34.67.

22. Based on the premium on a recent comparable transaction, Logan's best estimate of the takeover premium for Durtech is *closest* to:
    A. 19.9%.
    B. 23.9%.
    C. 35.8%.

23. Using comparable transaction analysis, Logan's estimate of the fair acquisition value per share for Durtech is *closest* to:
    A. $35.52.
    B. $42.59.
    C. $44.00.

24. The *best* justification for Logan's conclusion concerning possible government antitrust action is that:
    A. the post- and pre-merger HHI are both between 1000 and 1800.
    B. the change in the HHI is 100 or more and the post-merger HHI is between 1000 and 1800.
    C. the change in the HHI is 100 or more and the pre-merger HHI is between 1000 and 1800.

SOLUTIONS

CHAPTER 1

CORPORATE GOVERNANCE

SOLUTIONS

1. C is correct. Corporate governance is the system of principles, policies, procedures, and clearly defined responsibilities and accountabilities used by stakeholders to overcome the conflicts of interest inherent in the corporate form.

2. B is correct. Members of the board of directors serve as agents for the owners, the shareholders, a mechanism designed to represent the investors and to ensure that their interests are being well-served. An effective corporate governance system helps ensure that directors are aligned with shareholders' interests rather than management's interests.

3. A is correct. The board of directors has the responsibility to establish long-term strategic objectives for the company with a goal of ensuring that the best interests of shareholders come first and that the company's obligations to others are met in a timely and complete manner.

4. C is correct. Flagging items such as egregious use of insider transactions is least likely to be useful in assessing the quality of the corporate governance system. While egregious use of insider transactions is problematic, financial disclosures and related notes in regulatory filings are the source for analysts in researching such transactions.

5. C is correct. The objectives of an effective corporate governance system do not include ensuring complete transparency in disclosures regarding operations, performance, risk, and financial position. This is an attribute of an effective corporate governance system, not an objective.

6. A is correct. Fairness and equitable treatment in all dealings between managers, directors, and shareholders is a core attribute of an effective corporate governance system, not fairness and accuracy in identifying inherent conflicts of interest.

7. C is correct. An effective corporate governance system does not address conflicts of interest between managers and institutional analysts.

8. B is correct. There is no single system of effective corporate governance that applies to all firms worldwide. Different industries and economic systems, legal and regulatory environments, and cultural differences may affect the characteristics of an effective corporate governance system for a particular company.

9. C is correct. Interlocking directorships may be indicative of lack of independence. The lack of interlocking directorships does not indicate lack of independence.

10. A is correct. By establishing corporate values and an effective governance structure, the board attempts to ensure that the hedge fund's proxy voting is in the best interest of the shareholders of Zero.

11. A is correct. The board has omitted to address the potential conflicts of interest between managing the firm's hedge fund and mutual fund businesses. A failure to address this potential conflict of interest is a corporate governance shortcoming.

12. B is correct. The issue is that the directors may identify with the managers' interests rather than those of the shareholders. By eliminating or mitigating the conflicts of interests between managers and shareholders, the impact of this potential misidentification by the board is eliminated or mitigated.

13. A is correct. The two major objectives of corporate governance are to eliminate or mitigate conflicts of interest and to ensure the efficient and productive use of assets. The consultant has not yet reviewed for the efficient and productive use of assets.

14. C is correct. The most critical activity not yet performed by the consultant is the review to evaluate the quality and extent of financial information provided to investors. The consultant has performed the preliminary step of reviewing regulatory filings but has not yet evaluated the quality and extent of financial information provided.

15. A is correct. The two major objectives of corporate governance are to eliminate or mitigate conflicts of interest, particularly between managers and shareholders, and to ensure the efficient and productive use of assets in the best interests of the company's investors and other stakeholders.

16. B is correct. The Wall Street analyst is concerned with conflicts of interest. AMC should establish a corporate governance system that overcomes inherent conflicts of interest.

17. B is correct. The Wall Street analyst failed to consider the core attribute of fairness and equitable treatment in all dealings among managers, directors, and shareholders.

18. B is correct. The failure to disclose executive perquisites potentially reflects poor quality of the governance system.

19. C is correct. The board of directors has failed to meet regularly (meetings six months apart) to perform its duties.

CHAPTER 2

CAPITAL BUDGETING

SOLUTIONS

1. C is correct.

$$NPV = -50,000 + \frac{15,000}{1.08} + \frac{15,000}{1.08^2} + \frac{20,000}{1.08^3} + \frac{10,000}{1.08^4} + \frac{5,000}{1.08^5}$$

$$NPV = -50,000 + 13,888.89 + 12,860.08 + 15,876.64 + 7,350.30 + 3,402.92$$

$$NPV = -50,000 + 53,378.83 = 3,378.83$$

The IRR, found with a financial calculator, is 10.88%.

2. C is correct.

Year	0	1	2	3	4	5
Cash flow	−50,000	15,000	15,000	20,000	10,000	5,000
Cumulative cash flow	−50,000	−35,000	−20,000	0	10,000	15,000
Discounted cash flow	−50,000	13,888.89	12,860.08	15,876.64	7,350.30	3,402.92
Cumulative DCF	−50,000	−36,111.11	−23,251.03	−7,374.38	−24.09	3,378.83

As the table shows, the cumulative cash flow offsets the initial investment in exactly three years. The payback period is three years. The discounted payback period is between four and five years. The discounted payback period is four years plus 24.09/3,402.92 = 0.007 of the fifth year cash flow, or 4.007 = 4.01 years. The discounted payback period is 4.01 − 3.00 = 1.01 years longer than the payback period.

3. B is correct.

$$NPV = \sum_{t=0}^{3} \frac{CF_t}{(1+r)^t} = -100 + \frac{40}{1.20} + \frac{80}{1.20^2} + \frac{120}{1.20^3} = \$58.33$$

4. C is correct. The IRR can be found using a financial calculator or with trial and error. Using trial and error, the total PV is equal to zero if the discount rate is 28.79%.

Year	Cash Flow	Present Value			
		28.19%	28.39%	28.59%	28.79%
0	−150,000	−150,000	−150,000	−150,000	−150,000
1	100,000	78,009	77,888	77,767	77,646
2	120,000	73,025	72,798	72,572	72,346
Total		1,034	686	338	−8

A more precise IRR of 28.7854% has a total PV closer to zero.

5. A is correct. The NPV $= -750 + \sum_{t=1}^{7} \frac{175}{1.10^t} = -750 + 851.97 = 101.97$ million won.

The IRR, found with a financial calculator, is 14.02%. (The PV is -750, N $= 7$, and PMT $= 175$.)

6. B is correct.

Year	0	1	2	3	4	5	6	7
Cash flow	−750	175	175	175	175	175	175	175
Cumulative cash flow	−750	−575	−400	−225	−50	125	300	475

The payback period is between four and five years. The payback period is four years plus $50/175 = 0.29$ of the fifth year cash flow, or 4.29 years.

Year	0	1	2	3	4	5	6	7
Cash flow	−750	175	175	175	175	175	175	175
Discounted cash flow	−750	159.09	144.63	131.48	119.53	108.66	98.78	89.80
Cumulative DCF	−750	−590.91	−446.28	−314.80	−195.27	−86.61	12.17	101.97

The discounted payback period is between five and six years. The discounted payback period is five years plus $86.61/98.78 = 0.88$ of the sixth year cash flow, or 5.88 years.

7. C is correct.

The present value of future cash flows is PV $= \frac{2,000}{0.08} = 25,000$.

The profitability index is PI $= \frac{PV}{Investment} = \frac{25,000}{20,000} = 1.25$.

8. C is correct.

$$PV = \sum_{t=1}^{7} \frac{115}{1.10^t} + \frac{50}{1.10^7} = 585.53 \text{ million euros}$$

$$PI = \frac{585.53}{375} = 1.56$$

9. B is correct. The IRR would stay the same because both the initial outlay and the after-tax cash flows double, so that the return on each dollar invested remains the same. All of the cash flows and their present values double. The difference between total present value of the future cash flows and the initial outlay (the NPV) also doubles.

10. A is correct. If the cumulative cash flow in one year equals the outlay and additional cash flows are not very large, this scenario is possible. For example, assume the outlay is 100, the cash flow in Year 1 is 100, and the cash flow in Year 2 is 5. The required return is 10%. This project would have a payback of 1.0 year, an NPV of –4.96, and an IRR of 4.77%.

11. A is correct. The vertical intercept changes from 60 to 65 (NPV when cost of capital is 0%), and the horizontal intercept (IRR, when NPV equals zero) changes from 21.86% to 20.68%.

12. C is correct. When valuing mutually exclusive projects, the decision should be made with the NPV method because this method uses the most realistic discount rate, namely the opportunity cost of funds. In this example, the reinvestment rate for the NPV method (here 10 percent) is more realistic than the reinvestment rate for the IRR method (here 21.86% or 18.92%).

13. B is correct. For these projects, a discount rate of 13.16% would yield the same NPV for both (an NPV of 6.73).

14. C is correct. Discount rates of 0% and approximately 61.8% both give a zero NPV.

Rate	0%	20%	40%	60%	61.8%	80%	100%
NPV	0.00	4.40	3.21	0.29	0.00	−3.02	−6.25

15. A is correct. The crossover rate is the discount rate at which the NPV profiles for two projects cross; it is the only point where the NPVs of the projects are the same.

16. B is correct. The vertical axis represents a discount rate of zero. The point where the profile crosses the vertical axis is simply the sum of the cash flows.

17. C is correct. The horizontal axis represents an NPV of zero. By definition, the project's IRR equals an NPV of zero.

18. B is correct. Costs to finance the project are taken into account when the cash flows are discounted at the appropriate cost of capital; including interest costs in the cash flows would result in double-counting the cost of debt.

19. C is correct.

$$\text{Outlay} = \text{FCInv} + \text{NWCInv} - \text{Sal}_0 + T(\text{Sal}_0 - B_0)$$

$$\text{Outlay} = (350{,}000 + 110{,}000) + 73{,}000 - 0 + 0 = \$533{,}000$$

The installed cost is $\$350{,}000 + \$110{,}000 = \$460{,}000$, so the annual depreciation is $\$460{,}000/5 = \$92{,}000$. The annual after-tax operating cash flow for Years 1–5 is

$$CF = (S - C - D)(1 - T) + D = (265{,}000 - 83{,}000 - 92{,}000)(1 - 0.40) + 92{,}000$$

$$CF = \$146{,}000$$

The terminal year after-tax non-operating cash flow in Year 5 is

$$\text{TNOCF} = \text{Sal}_5 + \text{NWCInv} - T(\text{Sal}_5 - B_5) = 85{,}000 + 73{,}000 - 0.40(85{,}000 - 0)$$

$$\text{TNOCF} = \$124{,}000$$

The NPV is

$$\text{NPV} = -533{,}000 + \sum_{t=1}^{5} \frac{146{,}000}{1.10^t} + \frac{124{,}000}{1.10^5} = \$97{,}449$$

20. B is correct. The additional annual depreciation is $100,000/8 = $12,500. The depreciation tax savings is 0.40 ($12,500) = $5,000. The change in project NPV is

$$-100{,}000 + \sum_{t=1}^{8} \frac{5{,}000}{(1.10)^t} = -100{,}000 + 26{,}675 = -\$73{,}325$$

21. C is correct. Financing costs are not subtracted from the cash flows for either the NPV or the IRR. The effects of financing costs are captured in the discount rate used.

22. C is correct. The annual depreciation charge is $400,000/10 = $40,000. The after-tax operating cash flow in Year 1 should be

$$\text{CF} = (S - C - D)(1 - T) + D$$

$$= (240{,}000 - 110{,}000 - 40{,}000)(1 - 0.30) + 40{,}000$$

$$= 63{,}000 + 40{,}000 = \$103{,}000$$

23. C is correct. The terminal year after-tax non-operating cash flow is

$$\text{TNOCF} = \text{Sal}_5 + \text{NWCInv} - T(\text{Sal}_5 - B_5)$$

$$= 21 + 8 - 0.40(21 - 15) = £26.6 \text{ million}$$

24. C is correct. The investment outlay is

$$\text{Outlay} = \text{FCInv} + \text{NWCInv} - \text{Sal}_0 + T(\text{Sal}_0 - B_0)$$

$$= (360{,}000 + 40{,}000) + 60{,}000 - 0 + 0 = \$460{,}000$$

25. A is correct. Depreciation will be $400,000/5 = $80,000 per year. The annual after-tax operating cash flow is

$$\text{CF} = (S - C - D)(1 - T) + D$$

$$= [0 - (-140{,}000) - 80{,}000](1 - 0.40) + 80{,}000 = \$116{,}000$$

26. B is correct. The terminal year non-operating cash flow is

$$\text{TNOCF} = \text{Sal}_5 + \text{NWCInv} - T(\text{Sal}_5 - B_5)$$

$$= 120{,}000 + 60{,}000 - 0.40(120{,}000 - 0) = \$132{,}000$$

27. C is correct. The value of the depreciation tax savings is increased, and the value of the real after-tax interest expense is also increased. Due to the lower inflation, the value has increased (essentially discounting at a lower rate).
28. A is correct. The statement is correct for sensitivity analysis, but not for scenario analysis (in which several input variables are changed for each scenario).
29. B is correct. Either the least-common multiple of lives or the equivalent annual annuity approach should be used (both use the NPV, not the IRR). Concept 4 is correct as given.
30. C is correct. The problem gives EBIT, not EBITDA.

$$CF = (S - C - D)(1 - T) + D = 50(1 - 0.3) + 50 = €85 \text{ each year.}$$

31. A is correct. Economic income is the cash flow plus the change in value, or economic income is the cash flow minus the economic depreciation (we will use the second expression):

$$V_0 = \frac{85}{1.12} + \frac{85}{1.12^2} = 143.65 \quad V_1 = \frac{85}{1.12} = 75.89 \quad V_2 = 0$$

$$\text{Economic income (Year 1)} = CF1 - (V_0 - V_1)$$

$$= 85 - (143.65 - 75.89)$$

$$= 85 - 67.76 = €17.24$$

$$\text{Economic income (Year 2)} = CF_2 - (V_1 - V_2)$$

$$= 85 - (75.89 - 0)$$

$$= 85 - 75.89 = €9.11$$

32. C is correct.

$$EP = NOPAT - \$WACC = EBIT(1 - T) - WACC \times Capital$$

$$EP(Year1) = 50(1 - 0.30) - 0.12(100) = 35 - 12 = €23$$

$$EP(Year2) = 50(1 - 0.30) - 0.12(50) = 35 - 6 = €29$$

$$MVA = \frac{EP(Year1)}{1 + WACC} + \frac{EP(Year2)}{(1 + WACC)^2} = \frac{23}{1.12} + \frac{29}{1.12^2} = €43.65$$

(An alternative way to get MVA is simply to find the NPV of the investment project.)
33. B is correct. The way to solve the problem is to calculate the equivalent annual annuity and choose the service life with the lowest annual cost.
    For a two-year service life, the NPV is

$$NPV = -40,000 + \frac{-12,000}{1.10^1} + \frac{-15,000}{1.10^2} + \frac{20,000}{1.10^2} = -46,776.86$$

The EAA (PV $= -46,776.86$, $N = 2$, and $i = 10\%$) is $-26,952.38$.

For a three-year service life, the NPV is

$$\text{NPV} = -40{,}000 + \frac{-12{,}000}{1.10^1} + \frac{-15{,}000}{1.10^2} + \frac{-20{,}000}{1.10^3} + \frac{17{,}000}{1.10^3} = -65{,}559.73$$

The EAA (PV $= -65{,}559.73$, $N = 3$, and $i = 10\%$) is $-26{,}362.54$.
For a four-year service life, the NPV is

$$\text{NPV} = -40{,}000 + \frac{-12{,}000}{1.10^1} + \frac{-15{,}000}{1.10^2} + \frac{-20{,}000}{1.10^3} + \frac{-25{,}000}{1.10^4} + \frac{12{,}000}{1.10^4}$$

$$= -87{,}211.26$$

The EAA (PV $= -87{,}211.26$, $N = 4$, and $i = 10\%$) is $-27{,}512.61$.
The three-year service life has the lowest annual cost. Laroche should replace the vans every three years.

34. A is correct. To help the selection process, use the profitability index (PI) for each project, which shows the total present value per dollar invested.

Project	Outlay	PV of Future Cash Flows	NPV	PI	PI Rank
1	31	44	13	1.419	1
2	15	21	6	1.400	2
3	12	16.5	4.5	1.375	(tie) 3
4	10	13	3	1.300	6
5	8	11	3	1.375	(tie) 3
6	6	8	2	1.333	5

Try to incorporate the high-PI projects into the budget using trial and error. These trials include the following:

Set of Projects	Total Outlay	Total NPV
1 and 5	39	16
2, 3, and 4	37	13.5
2, 3, and 5	35	13.5
2, 4, 5, and 6	39	14

Among the sets of projects suggested, the optimal set is the one with the highest NPV, provided its total outlay does not exceed C\$40 million. The set consisting of Projects 1 and 5 produces the highest NPV.

35. B is correct.
If demand is "high," the NPV is

$$\text{NPV} = -190 + \sum_{t=1}^{10} \frac{40}{1.10^t} = \text{C\$55.783 million}$$

If demand is "low," the NPV is

$$\text{NPV} = -190 + \sum_{t=1}^{10} \frac{20}{1.10^t} = -\text{C\$67.109 million}$$

The expected NPV is $0.50(55.783) + 0.50(-67.109) = -\text{C\$5.663 million}$.

36. B is correct. Assume we are at time $= 1$. The NPV of the expansion (at time 1) if demand is "high" is

$$\text{NPV} = -190 + \sum_{t=1}^{9} \frac{40}{1.10^t} = \text{C\$40.361 million}$$

The NPV of the expansion (at time 1) if demand is "low" is

$$\text{NPV} = -190 + \sum_{t=1}^{9} \frac{20}{1.10^t} = -\text{C\$74.820 million}$$

The optimal decision is to expand if demand is "high" and not expand if "low."

Because the expansion option is exercised only when its value is positive, which happens 50 percent of the time, the expected value of the expansion project, at time zero, is

$$\text{NPV} = \frac{1}{1.10} 0.50(40.361) = \text{C\$18.346 million}$$

The total NPV of the initial project and the expansion project is

$$\text{NPV} = -\text{C\$5.663 million} + \text{C\$18.346 million} = \text{C\$12.683 million}$$

The optional expansion project, handled optimally, adds sufficient value to make this a positive NPV project.

37. A is correct. Both suggestions are bad. In valuing projects, expected cash flows should be discounted at required rates of return that reflect their risk, not at a risk-free rate that ignores risk. Even though both options cannot be simultaneously exercised, they can both add value. If demand is high, you can exercise the growth option, and if demand is low, you can exercise the abandonment option.

38. B is correct. Both suggestions are good. Choosing projects with high IRRs might cause the company to concentrate on short-term projects that reduce the NPV of the company. Whenever the project risk differs from the company risk, a project-specific required rate of return should be used.

39. C is correct. The after-tax operating cash flow for each of the next three years is $\$20,000 + \$40,000 = \$60,000$. The book value in three years will be $\$380,000$ (the original cost less three years' depreciation). So the terminal year after-tax non-operating cash flow will be $\text{Sal}_3 - 0.30(\text{Sal}_3 - \$380,000)$, where Sal_3 is the selling price. For a 15% return, the PV of future cash flows must equal the investment:

$$500,000 = \frac{60,000}{1.15} + \frac{60,000}{1.15^2} + \frac{60,000}{1.15^3} + \frac{\text{Sal}_3 - 0.30(\text{Sal}_3 - 380,000)}{1.15^3}$$

There are several paths to follow to solve for Sal_3.

$$363,006.5 = \frac{Sal_3 - 0.30(Sal_3 - 380,000)}{1.15^3}$$

$$Sal_3 - 0.30(Sal_3 - 380,000) = 552,087.5$$

$$0.70Sal_3 = 438,087.5$$

$$Sal_3 = \$625,839$$

40. A is correct. The cash flows (in \$ million) for the 5-year gas project are as follows:

Time	Outlays	After-Tax Operating Cash Flows	Total After-Tax Cash Flows
0	6.0	0.0	−6.0
1	1.0	0.5	−0.5
2	0.0	4.0	4.0
3	0.0	4.0	4.0
4	0.0	4.0	4.0
5	5.0	4.0	−1.0

Given the required rate of return of 18%, the NPV can be calculated as:

$$NPV = -6.0 + \frac{-0.5}{1.18} + \frac{4.0}{1.18^2} + \frac{4.0}{1.18^3} + \frac{4.0}{1.18^4} + \frac{-1.0}{1.18^5}$$

$$NPV = \$509,579$$

Similarly, the IRR can be calculated:

$$-6.0 + \frac{-0.5}{1 + r} + \frac{4.0}{(1 + r)^2} + \frac{4.0}{(1 + r)^3} + \frac{4.0}{(1 + r)^4} + \frac{-1.0}{(1 + r)^5} = 0$$

Solving for r with a financial calculator or spreadsheet software will yield 21.4% for the internal rate of return. Note that in spite of the fact that we are dealing with a nonconventional cash flow pattern, the IRR has a unique solution. The NPV profile declines as the required rate of return increases, and the NPV value crosses the x-axis (required rate of return) only one time, at 21.4%.

41. C is correct. Because the mutually exclusive projects have unequal lives, the EAA should be used instead of the NPV. The NPV and EAA for the Pinto grinder are correct. For the Bolten grinder, the NPV is

$$NPV = -125,000 + \sum_{t=1}^{4} \frac{47,000}{1.10^t} + \frac{20,000}{1.10^4} = 37,644$$

To find the Bolten EAA, take the NPV for Bolten and annualize it for four years ($N = 4$, PV = 37,644, and $i = 10\%$). The Bolten EAA is $11,876. Consequently, the Pinto grinder has the better EAA of $12,341.

42. B is correct. Goldberg's first comment is wrong. A project should be abandoned in the future only when its abandonment value is more than the discounted value of the remaining cash flows. Goldberg's second comment is correct.

43. A is correct. The $10 million original cost is a sunk cost and not relevant. The correct investment is today's opportunity cost, the market value today. The correct discount rate is the project's required rate of return.

44. C is correct. Even if they are the same size, a short-term project with a high IRR can have a lower NPV than a longer-term project. The immediate impact on EPS does not capture the full effect of the cash flows over the project's entire life.

45. A is correct. The annual depreciation charge for Years 1–6 is $1.5/6 = 0.25$. Annual after-tax operating cash flows for Years 1–6 are:

$$CF = (S - C - D)(1 - T) + D$$

$$CF = [0.10 - (-0.25) - 0.25](1 - 0.40) + 0.25$$

$$CF = 0.06 + 0.25 = €0.31 \text{ billion}$$

Annual after-tax operating cash flows for Years 7–12 are:

$$CF = (S - C - D)(1 - T) + D$$

$$CF = [0.10 - (-0.25) - 0](1 - 0.40) + 0$$

$$CF = €0.21 \text{ billion}$$

46. B is correct.
   Outlay at time zero is:

$$\text{Outlay} = FCInv + NWCInv - Sal_0 + T(Sal_0 - B_0)$$

$$\text{Outlay} = 1.50 + 0.40 - 0 + 0 = €1.90 \text{ billion.}$$

Terminal year after-tax non-operating cash flow is

$$TNOCF = Sal_{12} + NWCInv - T(Sal_{12} - B_{12})$$

$$TNOCF = 0.50 + 0.40 - 0.40(0.50 - 0) = €0.70 \text{ billion}$$

47. B is correct. The cash flows, computed in the first two questions, are as follows:

Time 0	−€1.90 billion
Time 1–6	€0.31 billion
Time 7–12	€0.21 billion
Time 12	€0.70 billion

The NPV is

$$NPV = -1.90 + \sum_{t=1}^{6} \frac{0.31}{1.12^t} + \sum_{t=7}^{12} \frac{0.21}{1.12^t} + \frac{0.70}{1.12^{12}}$$

$$NPV = -1.90 + 1.2745 + 0.4374 + 0.1797 = -€0.0084 \text{ billion} \approx -€0.01 \text{ billion}$$

48. A is correct. Accelerated depreciation shifts depreciation expense toward the earlier years so that first-year operating income after taxes will be lower. However, because depreciation is a noncash expense, it must be added back to operating income after taxes in order to obtain after-tax operating cash flow. This process shifts cash flows from later years to earlier years, increasing the NPV.

49. C is correct. The outlay is lower by €0.24, which will decrease the annual depreciation by €0.04 for the first six years. The annual additional taxes from the loss of the depreciation tax shelter are €0.04(0.40) = €0.016. The after-tax cash flows are higher by €0.24 at time zero (because of the smaller investment) and lower by €0.016 for the first six years. The NPV increases by

$$NPV = +0.24 - \sum_{t=1}^{6} \frac{0.016}{1.12^t} = 0.24 - 0.0658 = 0.1742 = €0.17 \text{ billion}$$

50. A is correct. Both of the supervisor's comments are incorrect. Because the Bayonne Pharma project is a conventional project (an outflow followed by inflows), the multiple IRR problem cannot occur. The EAA is preferred over the NPV when dealing with mutually exclusive projects with differing lives, a scenario which is not relevant for this decision. The Bayonne Pharma project is free-standing, so the NPV approach is appropriate.

51. B is correct.

Economic income = Cash flow − Economic depreciation

Economic income (Year 1) = $CF_1 - (V_0 - V_1)$

After-tax operating cash flow (CF) = $(S - C - D)(1 - T) + D +$ After-tax salvage = $EBIT(1 - T) + D +$ After-tax salvage

Year	1	2	3	4	5
EBIT	30,000	40,000	50,000	60,000	40,000
EBIT(1 − 0.40)	18,000	24,000	30,000	36,000	24,000
D	40,000	40,000	40,000	40,000	40,000
After-tax salvage					12,000
CF	58,000	64,000	70,000	76,000	76,000

$CF_1 = 58,000$

$$V_0 = \frac{58,000}{1.12} + \frac{64,000}{1.12^2} + \frac{70,000}{1.12^3} + \frac{76,000}{1.12^4} + \frac{76,000}{1.12^5} = 244,054.55$$

$$V_1 = \frac{64,000}{1.12} + \frac{70,000}{1.12^2} + \frac{76,000}{1.12^3} + \frac{76,000}{1.12^4} = 215,341.10$$

Economic income (Year 1) = 58,000 − (244,054.55 − 215,341.10)

Economic income (Year 1) = 58,000 − 28,713.45 = 29,286.55

52. B is correct.

$$EP = NOPAT - \$WACC$$

$$NOPAT = EBIT(1 - Tax\ rate) = 30,000(1 - 0.40) = 18,000$$

$$\$WACC = WACC \times Capital = 0.12(200,000) = 24,000$$

$$EP = 18,000 - 24,000 = -6,000$$

53. A is correct.

$$RI_t = NI_t - r_e B_{t-1}$$

$$RI_1 = 11,899 - 0.19(77,973) = 11,899 - 14,815 = -2,916$$

54. C is correct. The value of equity is the PV of cash distributions to equity:

$$PV = \frac{37,542}{1.19} + \frac{39,536}{1.19^2} + \frac{41,201}{1.19^3} + \frac{42,496}{1.19^4} + \frac{40,375}{1.19^5} = 122,027$$

55. B is correct. Robinson's first statement is wrong. The value of an asset is the present value of its future cash flows. Economic income each year is the cash flow minus economic depreciation: $EI = CF - ED$. For this company, which is declining in value each year, the economic depreciation is positive and EI is less than CF each year. Consequently, the present value of economic income (EI) will be less than the present value of future cash flows (CF). Robinson's second statement is correct.

56. B is correct. Market value added is equal to the present value of EP. Its value, however, is not equal to the book value of equity. The calculation of MVA is shown here:

Year	1	2	3	4	5*
EBIT	30,000	40,000	50,000	60,000	60,000
NOPAT = EBIT(1 − 0.40)	18,000	24,000	30,000	36,000	36,000
Capital (beginning)	200,000	160,000	120,000	80,000	40,000
$WACC = 0.12 × Capital	24,000	19,200	14,400	9,600	4,800
EP = NOPAT − $WACC	−6,000	4,800	15,600	26,400	31,200

*The fifth-year figures include the effects of salvage. Before-tax salvage of 20,000 [= 12,000/(1 − 0.40)] is added to EBIT. The after-tax salvage of 12,000 is included in NOPAT.

$$MVA = \frac{-6,000}{1.12} + \frac{4,800}{1.12^2} + \frac{15,600}{1.12^3} + \frac{26,400}{1.12^4} + \frac{26,400}{1.12^5} = 44,054.55$$

COST OF CAPITAL

SOLUTIONS

1. B is correct. The cost of equity is defined as the rate of return required by stockholders.
2. B is correct. Debt is generally less costly than preferred or common stock. The cost of debt is further reduced if interest expense is tax deductible.
3. C is correct. First calculate the growth rate using the sustainable growth calculation, and then calculate the cost of equity using the rearranged dividend discount model:

$$g = (1 - \text{Dividend payout ratio})(\text{Return on equity}) = (1 - 0.30)(15\%) = 10.5\%$$

$$r_e = (D_1/P_0) + g = (\$2.30/\$45) + 10.50\% = 15.61\%$$

4. C is correct. $FV = \$1,000$; $PMT = \$40$; $N = 10$; $PV = \$900$
   Solve for i. The six-month yield, i, is 5.3149%.

$$\text{YTM} = 5.3149\% \times 2 = 10.62985\%$$

$$r_d(1 - t) = 10.62985\%(1 - 0.38) = 6.5905\%$$

5. C is correct. The bond rating approach depends on knowledge of the company's rating and can be compared with yields on bonds in the public market.
6. B is correct. The company can issue preferred stock at 6.5%.

$$P_p = \$1.75/0.065 = \$26.92$$

7. B is correct. Cost of equity $= D_1/P_0 + g = \$1.50/\$30 + 7\% = 5\% + 7\% = 12\%$

$$D/(D + E) = 0.8033/1.8033 = 0.445$$

$$\text{WACC} = [(0.445)(0.08)(1 - 0.4)] + [(0.555)(0.12)] = 8.8\%$$

8. B is correct. The weighted average cost of capital, using weights derived from the current capital structure, is the best estimate of the cost of capital for the average risk project of a company.
9. C is correct.

$$w_d = \$63/(\$220 + 63) = 0.223$$

$$w_e = \$220/(\$220 + 63) = 0.777$$

10. B is correct. Asset risk does not change with a higher debt-to-equity ratio. Equity risk rises with higher debt.

11. B is correct. The debt-to-equity ratio of the new product should be used when making the adjustment from the asset beta, derived from the comparables, to the equity beta of the new product.

12. B is correct.

Capital structure:

Market value of debt: $FV = \$10,000,000$; $PMT = \$400,000$, $N = 10$, $I/YR = 13.65\%$. Solving for PV gives the answer $\$7,999,688$.

Market value of equity: 1.2 million shares outstanding @ $\$10 = \$12,000,000$

Market value of debt	$7,999,688	40%
Market value of equity	12,000,000	60%
Total capital	$19,999,688	100%

To raise $7.5 million of new capital while maintaining the same capital structure, the company would issue $7.5 million $\times$ 40% = $3.0 million in bonds, which results in a before-tax rate of 16%.

$$r_d(1 - t) = 0.16(1 - 0.3) = 0.112 \text{ or } 11.2\%$$

$$r_e = 0.03 + 2.2 \ (0.10 - 0.03) = 0.184 \text{ or } 18.4\%$$

$$\text{WACC} = [0.40(0.112)] + [0.6(0.184)] = 0.0448 + 0.1104 = 0.1552 \text{ or } 15.52\%$$

13. B is correct. $r_e = 0.0425 + (1.3)(0.0482) = 0.1052$ or 10.52%
14. B is correct. WACC = $[(€900/€3,300) \ 0.0925 \ (1 - 0.375)] + [(€2,400/€3,300)(0.1052)] = 0.0923$ or 9.23%
15. A is correct. Asset beta = Unlevered beta = $1.3/(1 + [(1 - 0.375)(€900/€2,400)] = 1.053$
16. C is correct. Project beta = $1.053 \times \{1 + [(1 - 0.375)(€80/€20)]\} = 1.053(3.5) = 3.686$
17. C is correct. $r_e = 0.0425 + 3.686(0.0482 + 0.0188) = 0.2895$ or 28.95%
18. C is correct.

Cost of equity without the country risk premium:

$$r_e = 0.0425 + 3.686(0.0482) = 0.2202 \text{ or } 22.02\%$$

Cost of equity with the country risk premium:

$$r_e = 0.0425 + 3.686(0.0482 + 0.0188) = 0.2895 \text{ or } 28.95\%$$

Weighted average cost of capital without the country risk premium:

$$\text{WACC} = [0.80(0.0925)(1 - 0.375)] + [0.20(0.2202)] = 0.04625 + 0.04404$$
$$= 0.09038 \text{ or } 9.03\%$$

Weighted average cost of capital with the country risk premium:

$$\text{WACC} = [0.80(0.0925)(1 - 0.375)] + [0.20(0.2895)] = 0.04625 + 0.0579$$
$$= 0.1042 \text{ or } 10.42\%$$

NPV without the country risk premium:

$$NPV = \frac{€48 \text{ million}}{(1 + 0.0903)^1} + \frac{€52 \text{ million}}{(1 + 0.0903)^2} + \frac{€54.4 \text{ million}}{(1 + 0.0903)^3} - €100 \text{ million}$$

$$= €44.03 \text{ million} + 43.74 \text{ million} + 41.97 \text{ million} - €100 \text{ million} = €29.74 \text{ million}$$

NPV with the country risk premium:

$$NPV = \frac{€48 \text{ million}}{(1 + 0.1042)^1} + \frac{€52 \text{ million}}{(1 + 0.1042)^2} + \frac{€54.4 \text{ million}}{(1 + 0.1042)^3} - €100 \text{ million}$$

$$= €43.47 \text{ million} + 42.65 \text{ million} + 40.41 \text{ million} - €100 \text{ million} = €26.54 \text{ million}$$

19. B is correct.
    Asset betas: $\beta_{equity}/[1 + (1 - t)(D/E)]$

$$\text{Relevant} = 1.702/[1 + (0.77)(0)] = 1.702$$

$$\text{ABJ} = 2.8/[1 + (0.77)(0.003)] = 2.7918$$

$$\text{Opus} = 3.4/1 + [(0.77)(0.013)] = 3.3663$$

20. C is correct. Weights are determined based on relative market values:

Pure-Play	Market Value of Equity in Billions	Proportion of Total
Relevant	$3.800	0.5490
ABJ	2.150	0.3106
Opus	0.972	0.1404
Total	$6.922	1.0000

$$\text{Weighted average beta} = (0.5490)(1.702) + (0.3106)(2.7918)$$
$$+ (0.1404)(3.3572) = 2.27$$

21. B is correct.

$$\text{Asset beta} = 2.27$$

$$\text{Levered beta} = 2.27\{1 + [(1 - 0.23)(0.01)]\} = 2.2875$$

$$\text{Cost of equity capital} = 0.0525 + (2.2875)(0.07) = 0.2126 \text{ or } 21.26\%$$

22. C is correct.
    For debt: FV = 2,400,000; PV = 2,156,000; $n = 10$; PMT = 150,000
    Solve for i. $i = 0.07748$. YTM = 15.5%
    Before-tax cost of debt = 15.5%
    Market value of equity = 1 million shares outstanding plus 1 million newly issued shares = 2 million shares at $8 = $16 million

Total market capitalization $= \$2.156$ million $+ \$16$ million $= \$18.156$ million
Levered beta $= 2.27\{1 + [(1 - 0.23)(2.156/16)]\} = 2.27\ (1.1038) = 2.5055$
Cost of equity $= 0.0525 + 2.5055(0.07) = 0.2279$ or 22.79%
Debt weight $= \$2.156/\$18.156 = 0.1187$
Equity weight $= \$16/\$18.156 = 0.8813$

$$
\begin{aligned}
\text{TagOn's MCC} &= [(0.1187)(0.155)(1 - 0.23)] + [(0.8813)(0.2279)] \\
&= 0.01417 + 0.20083 \\
&= 0.2150 \text{ or } 21.50\%
\end{aligned}
$$

23. A is correct. The relevant cost is the marginal cost of debt. The before-tax marginal cost of debt can be estimated by the yield to maturity on a comparable outstanding. After adjusting for tax, the after-tax cost is $7(1 - 0.4) = 7(0.6) = 4.2\%$.
24. C is correct. The expected return is the sum of the expected dividend yield plus expected growth. The expected growth is $(1 - 0.4)15\% = 9\%$. The expected dividend yield is $\$2.18/\$28 = 7.8\%$. The sum is 16.8%.
25. B is correct. Using the CAPM approach, $4\% + 1.3(9\%) = 15.7\%$.
26. C is correct. Inferring the asset beta for the public company: unlevered beta $= 1.75/ [1 + (1 - 0.35)(0.90)] = 1.104$. Relevering to reflect the target debt ratio of the private firm: levered beta $= 1.104 \times [1 + (1 - 0.30)(1.00)] = 1.877$.
27. C is correct. The country equity premium can be estimated as the sovereign yield spread times the volatility of the country's stock market relative to its bond market. Paragon's equity premium is $(10.5\% - 4.5\%) \times (35\%/25\%) = 6\% \times 1.4 = 8.40\%$.

CHAPTER 4

MEASURES OF LEVERAGE

SOLUTIONS

1. C is correct. The companies' degree of operating leverage should be the same, consistent with C. Sales risk refers to the uncertainty of the number of units produced and sold and the price at which units are sold. Business risk is the joint effect of sales risk and operating risk.

2. C is correct. The degree of operating leverage is the elasticity of operating earnings with respect to the number of units produced and sold. As an elasticity, the degree of operating leverage measures the sensitivity of operating earnings to a change in the number of units produced and sold.

3. C is correct. Because DOL is 4, if unit sales increase by 5%, Fulcrum's operating earnings are expected to increase by $4 \times 5\% = 20\%$. The calculation for DOL is:

$$\text{DOL} = \frac{(40 \text{ million})(\$100 - \$65)}{[(40 \text{ million})(\$100 - \$65)] - \$1.05 \text{ billion}}$$

$$= \frac{\$1.400 \text{ billion}}{\$1.400 \text{ billion} - \$1.05 \text{ billion}} = \frac{\$1.4}{\$0.35} = 4$$

4. C is correct. Business risk reflects operating leverage and factors that affect sales (such as those given).

5. B is correct. Grundlegend's degree of operating leverage is the same as Basic Company's, whereas Grundlegend's degree of total leverage and degree of financial leverage are higher.

6. B is correct.

$$\text{Operating breakeven units} = \frac{\text{¥}1,290 \text{ million}}{(\text{¥}3,529 - \text{¥}1,500)} = 635,781.173 \text{ units}$$

$$\text{Operating breakeven sales} = \text{¥}3,529 \times 635,781.173 \text{ units} = \text{¥}2,243,671,760$$

or

$$\text{Operating breakeven sales} = \frac{\text{¥}1,290 \text{ million}}{1 - (\text{¥}1,500/\text{¥}3,529)} = \text{¥}2,243,671,760$$

$$\text{Total breakeven} = \frac{\text{¥}1,290 \text{ million} + \text{¥}410 \text{ million}}{(\text{¥}3,529 - \text{¥}1,500)} = \frac{\text{¥}1,700 \text{ million}}{\text{¥}2,029} = 837,851.1582 \text{ units}$$

$$\text{Breakeven sales} = \text{¥}3,529 \times 837,851.1582 \text{ units} = \text{¥}2,956,776,737$$

or

$$\text{Breakeven sales} = \frac{\yen 1,700 \text{ million}}{1 - (\yen 1,500/\yen 3,529)} = \yen 2,956,776,737$$

7. A is correct. For The Gearing Company,

$$Q_{BE} = \frac{F + C}{P - V} = \frac{\$40 \text{ million} + \$20 \text{ million}}{\$200 - \$120} = 750,000$$

For Hebelkraft, Inc.,

$$Q_{BE} = \frac{F + C}{P - V} = \frac{\$90 \text{ million} + \$20 \text{ million}}{\$200 - \$100} = 1,100,000$$

8. C is correct. Sales risk is defined as uncertainty with respect to the price or quantity of goods and services sold. 4G has a higher standard deviation of unit sales than Qphone; in addition, 4G's standard deviation of unit sales stated as a fraction of its level of unit sales, at $25,000/1,000,000 = 0.025$, is greater than the comparable ratio for Qphone, $10,000/1,500,000 = 0.0067$.

9. B is correct. Business risk is associated with operating earnings. Operating earnings are affected by sales risk (uncertainty with respect to price and quantity) and operating risk (the operating cost structure and the level of fixed costs).

10. C is correct. Operating risk refers to the risk arising from the mix of fixed and variable costs.

11. B is correct.

$$DOL = \frac{Q(P - V)}{Q(P - V) - F}$$

$$\begin{array}{l} DOL @ \\ 1,000,000 \text{ units} \end{array} = \frac{1,000,000(\yen 108 - \yen 72)}{1,000,000(\yen 108 - \yen 72) - \yen 22,500,000} = 2.67$$

12. C is correct. Degree of financial leverage is

$$DFL = \frac{[Q(P - V) - F]}{[Q(P - V) - F - C]}$$

$$= \frac{1,000,000(\yen 108 - \yen 72) - \yen 22,500,000}{1,000,000(\yen 108 - \yen 72) - \yen 22,500,000 - \yen 9,000,000} = 3.00$$

13. B is correct. The degree of operating leverage of Qphone is 1.4. The percentage change in operating income is equal to the DOL times the percentage change in units sold; therefore:

$$\begin{array}{l} \text{Percentage change} \\ \text{in operating income} \end{array} = (DOL) \left(\begin{array}{l} \text{Percentage change} \\ \text{in units sold} \end{array} \right) = (1.4)(15\%) = 21\%$$

14. C is correct. The breakeven quantity is computed

$$Q_{BE} = \frac{F + C}{P - V} = \frac{(¥22,500,000 + ¥9,000,000)}{(¥108 - ¥72)} = 875,000$$

15. C is correct. 4G, Inc.'s degree of total leverage can be shown to equal 8, whereas Qphone Corp.'s degree of total leverage is only $DOL \times DFL = 1.4 \times 1.15 = 1.61$. Therefore, a 10% increase in unit sales will mean an 80% increase in net income for 4G, but only a 16.1% increase in net income for Qphone Corp. The calculation for 4G, Inc.'s DTL is

$$\begin{aligned} DTL &= \frac{Q(P - V)}{Q(P - V) - F - C} \\ &= \frac{1,000,000(¥108 - ¥72)}{1,000,000(¥108 - ¥72) - ¥22,500,000 - ¥9,000,000} = 8.00 \end{aligned}$$

16. A is correct. Degree of total leverage is defined as the percentage change in net income divided by the percentage change in units sold.

CHAPTER 5

CAPITAL STRUCTURE

SOLUTIONS

1. B is correct. Proposition I, or the capital structure irrelevance theorem, states that the level of debt versus equity in the capital structure has no effect on company value in perfect markets.

2. C is correct. The cost of equity rises with the use of debt in the capital structure (e.g., with increasing financial leverage).

3. C is correct.

$$0.10 = (0.50)(0.05)(1 - 0.20) + (0.50)r_e$$

$$r_e = 0.16 \text{ or } 16\%$$

4. C is correct. If the company's WACC increases as a result of taking on additional debt, the company has moved beyond the optimal capital range. The costs of financial distress may outweigh any tax benefits of the use of debt.

5. A is correct. The use of long-maturity debt is expected to be inversely related to the level of inflation.

6. A is correct. According to the pecking order theory, internally generated funds are preferable to both new equity and new debt. If internal financing is insufficient, managers next prefer new debt, and finally new equity.

7. B is correct. The static trade-off theory indicates that there is a trade-off between the tax shield from interest on debt and the costs of financial distress, leading to an optimal amount of debt in a company's capital structure.

8. A is correct. The market value of equity is ($30)(10,000,000) = $300,000,000. With the market value of debt equal to $100,000,000, the market value of the company is $100,000,000 + $300,000,000 = $400,000,000. Therefore, the company is $100,000,000/$400,000,000 = 0.25 or 25% debt financed.

9. B is correct. $r_d(1 - t) = 0.08(1 - 0.35) = 0.052 = 5.20\%$.

10. B is correct.

$$r_e = r_0 + (r_0 - r_d)(1 - t)\frac{D}{E}$$

$$= 0.103 + (0.103 - 0.08)(1 - 0.35)\left(\frac{\$100 \text{ million}}{\$300 \text{ million}}\right)$$

$$= 0.108 = 10.80\%$$

11. B is correct. Let $V = D + E$:

$$r_{WACC} = \left(\frac{D}{V}\right)r_d(1-t) + \left(\frac{E}{V}\right)r_e$$

At $D/V = 20\%$, $r_a = (0.2)(0.077)(1-0.35) + (0.8)(0.125) = 0.1100 = 11.00\%$

At $D/V = 30\%$, $r_a = (0.3)(0.084)(1-0.35) + (0.7)(0.130) = 0.1074 = 10.74\%$

At $D/V = 40\%$, $r_a = (0.4)(0.093)(1-0.35) + (0.6)(0.140) = 0.1082 = 10.82\%$

At $D/V = 50\%$, $r_a = (0.5)(0.104)(1-0.35) + (0.5)(0.160) = 0.1138 = 11.38\%$

12. A is correct. The after-tax cost of debt decreases as the marginal tax rate increases.
13. C is correct. If internally generated funds have already been fully used, the use of new debt may be optimal, according to the pecking order theory of capital structure.
14. B is correct.

$$V_L = \frac{\text{EBIT}(1-t)}{r_{WACC}}$$

Because $D/E = 0.60$ and $D = £2m$, then $E = £2m/(0.60) = £3,333,333$.
So, Value of company $(V_L) = D + E = £2,000,000 + £3,333,333 = £5,333,333$.
Because

$$V_L = \frac{\text{EBIT}(1-t)}{r_{WACC}} = \frac{(600,000)(1-0.30)}{r_{WACC}} = 5,333,333$$

So,

$$r_{WACC} = \frac{(600,000)(1-0.30)}{5,333,333} = 0.0787 = 7.87\%$$

15. C is correct.

$$r_e = r_0 + (r_0 - r_d)(1-t)\left(\frac{D}{E}\right), \quad \text{and} \quad r_{WACC} = \left(\frac{D}{V}\right)r_d(1-t) + \left(\frac{E}{V}\right)r_e$$

$$r_e = r_0 + (r_0 - r_d)(1-t)\left(\frac{D}{E}\right) = 10 + (10-6)(1-0.30)(0.60) = 10 + 1.68$$

$$= 11.68\%$$

Therefore,

$$r_{WACC} = \left(\frac{D}{V}\right)r_d(1-t) + \left(\frac{E}{V}\right)r_e = \left(\frac{0.6}{1.6}\right)(6)(1-0.30) + \left(\frac{1.0}{1.6}\right)(11.68)$$

$$= 1.58 + 7.30 = 8.88\%$$

16. B is correct. If Bema's degree of operating leverage declines relative to that of Aquarius, Bema's business risk will also decline relative to Aquarius's. All else being equal, this decline would be expected to *increase* Bema's market value relative to Aquarius (e.g., by decreasing Bema's cost of equity).

17. C is correct.

$$r_e = r_0 + (r_0 - r_d)(1 - t)\left(\frac{D}{E}\right)$$

$$V_U = \frac{\text{EBIT}(1 - t)}{r_0} = \frac{400{,}000(1 - 0.30)}{0.10} = 2{,}800{,}000$$

$V_L = V_U + tD = (2.8 \text{ million}) + (0.30)(1 \text{ million}) = 3.10 \text{ million}$

$E = V_L - D = (3.10 \text{ million}) - (1 \text{ million}) = 2.10 \text{ million}$

$r_e = r_0 + (r_0 - r_d)(1 - t)\left(\frac{D}{E}\right) = 10 + (10 - 6)(1 - 0.30)\left(\frac{1}{2.10}\right) = 10 + 1.33 = 11.33\%$

18. A is correct. The statement implies that Garth possesses a lower ability to assume debt than does Holte, all else being equal.

19. C is correct. According to the pecking order theory, managers prefer internal financing. If internal financing is not sufficient, managers next prefer debt, and finally equity.

CHAPTER 6

DIVIDENDS AND SHARE REPURCHASES: BASICS

SOLUTIONS

1. C is correct. A stock dividend is accounted for as a transfer of retained earnings to contributed capital.

2. C is correct. A reverse stock split would increase the price per share of the stock to a higher, more marketable range that could possibly increase the number of investors who would consider buying the stock.

3. A is correct. Both statements are incorrect. A stock dividend will decrease the price per share, all other things being equal. A stock split will reduce the price and earnings per share proportionately, leaving the price-to-earnings ratio the same.

4. A is correct. By reducing corporate cash, a cash dividend reduces the current ratio, whereas a stock dividend (whatever the size) has no effect on the current ratio.

5. The typical dividend chronology is:

Friday, 10 June	B. The declaration date is the day that the corporation issues a statement declaring a dividend.
Thursday, 23 June	E. The last day shares trade with the right to receive the dividend is the day before the ex-dividend date.
Friday, 24 June	D. The ex-dividend date is the first day that the stock trades "ex" (i.e., without) the dividend. If the stock is bought on the ex-dividend date, the seller (not the buyer) will receive the dividend.
Tuesday, 28 June	A. The holder-of-record date is the date that the company uses to document which shareholders will receive the dividend.
Sunday, 10 July	C. The payment date is the date that the company sends out its dividend checks.

6. A is correct. To receive the dividend, one must purchase before the ex-dividend date.

7. B is correct. The holder-of-record date, 30 October, is two business days after the ex-dividend date, 28 October.

8. C is correct. At the current market price, the company can repurchase 200,000 shares (£10 million/£50 = 200,000 shares). The company would have 800,000 shares outstanding after the repurchase (1 million shares − 200,000 shares = 800,000 shares).

EPS before the buyback is £2.00 (£2 million/1 million shares = £2.00). Total earnings after the buyback are the same because the company uses idle (nonearning) cash to purchase the shares, but the number of shares outstanding is reduced to 800,000. EPS increases to £2.50 (£2 million/800,000 shares = £2.50).

9. B is correct. If the P/E is 32, the earnings-to-price ratio (earnings yield or E/P) is 1/32 = 3.125%. When the cost of capital is greater than the earnings yield, earnings dilution will result from the buyback.

10. A is correct. The company's earnings yield (E/P) is $2/$40 = 0.05. When the earnings yield is greater than the after-tax cost of borrowed funds, EPS will increase if shares are repurchased using borrowed funds.

11. A is correct.

Total earnings before buyback: $4.00 × 3,100,000 shares = $12,400,000

Total amount of borrowing: $50 × 100,000 shares = $5,000,000

After-tax cost of borrowing the amount of funds needed: $5,000,000 × 0.06 = $300,000

Number of shares outstanding after buyback: 3,100,000 − 100,000 = 3,000,000

EPS after buyback: ($12,400,000 − $300,000)/3,000,000 shares = $4.03

The P/E before the buyback is $50/$4 = 12.5; thus, the E/P is 8%. The after-tax cost of debt is 6%; therefore, EPS will increase.

12. C is correct. The company's book value before the buyback is €850 million in assets − €250 million in liabilities = €600 million. Book value per share is €600 million/ 20 million = €30 per share. The buyback will reduce equity by 2 million shares at the prevailing market price of €30 per share. The book value of equity will be reduced to €600 million − €60 million = €540 million and the number of shares will be reduced to 18 million. €540 million/18 million = €30 book value per share. If the prevailing market price is equal to the book value per share at the time of the buyback, book value per share is unchanged.

13. C is correct. The prevailing market price is $2.00(20) = $40 per share; thus, the buyback would reduce equity by $40 million. Book value of equity before the buyback is $300 million. Book value of equity after the buyback would be $300 million − $40 million = $260 million. The number of shares outstanding after the buyback would be 9 million. Thus, book value per share after the buyback would be $260 million/9 million = $28.89.

14. C is correct. Of the three methods, only an authorized open market share repurchase plan allows the company the flexibility to time share repurchases to coincide with share price declines.

15. C is correct. For the two options to be equivalent with respect to shareholders' wealth, the amount of cash distributed, the taxation, and the information content must be the same for both options.

16. C is correct. When there are no taxes, there are no tax differences between dividends and capital gains. All other things being equal, the effect on shareholder wealth of a dividend and a share repurchase should be the same.

CHAPTER 7

DIVIDENDS AND SHARE REPURCHASES: ANALYSIS

SOLUTIONS

1. The appropriate matches are as follows:

Column A	Column B
1. Bird in the hand	a) Dividend policy matters
2. Homemade dividends	b) Dividend policy is irrelevant
3. High tax rates on dividends	a) Dividend policy matters

2. B is correct. The MM dividend theory assumes no taxes or transaction costs, but does not assume a clientele effect.

3. B is correct. The clientele effect implies that there are varying preferences for dividends among distinct investor groups.

4. C is correct. Because the clientele for PAT Company investors has the same tax rate (zero) for dividends and capital gains, the ex-dividend stock price of PAT should decline by the amount of the dividend to €40 − €1.50 = €38.50. She will purchase €150,000/€38.50 = 3,896 additional shares. This increases her total shares owned to 103,896. Chan's new share ownership is closest to 103,900.

5. B is correct. A decrease in the quarterly dividend rate is likely to signal negative information. A decrease is typically understood as signaling poor future business prospects.

6. B is correct. The effective tax rate can be computed as 1 minus the fraction of 1 unit of earnings that investors retain after all taxes, or $1 - (1 - 0.40)(1 - 0.30) = 0.58$ or 58% effective tax rate. Another way to obtain the solution: Corporate taxes $= 1.00 \times 0.40 = 0.40$ and personal taxes $= 0.60$ in dividends $\times 0.30 = 0.18$, so total tax $= 0.40 + 0.18 = 0.58$, a 58% effective rate.

7. A is correct. With low growth prospects, a company would typically have a high payout ratio, returning funds to its shareholders rather than retaining funds.

8. A is correct. The estimated dividend per share is $0.65.

$$\text{Previous DPS} = \$0.60$$

$$\text{Expected increase in EPS} = \$4 - \$3 = \$1$$

$$\text{Target payout ratio} = 0.25$$

$$\text{Five-year adjustment factor} = 1/5 = 0.2$$

$$\text{Expected DPS} = \text{Previous DPS} + (\text{Increase in EPS} \times \text{Target payout} \times \text{Adjustment factor})$$

$$= \$0.60 + (\$1.00 \times 0.25 \times 0.2)$$

$$= \$0.65$$

9. A is correct. Using the residual dividend policy, with a target debt/equity ratio of 40/60, 60% or $24 million of the $40 million in capital expenditures will be financed with equity; $30 million net income − $24 million retained earnings = $6 million for dividends.

10. B is correct. Choice A is consistent with a target payout ratio policy. Choice C is not correct, because the earnings increases described are not sustainable for the long term.

11. A is correct. When capital gains are taxed at lower rates than dividends are, investors may prefer companies that return cash to shareholders through share repurchases rather than dividends.

12. B is correct. Management sometimes undertakes share repurchases when it views shares as being undervalued in the marketplace.

13. B is correct. Earnings available for dividends = Earnings − Capital spending = $25 million − $15 million = $10 million; $10 million/$25 million = 40% dividend payout ratio.

14. C is correct. Shareholders would prefer that the company repurchase its shares instead of paying dividends when the tax rate on capital gains is lower than the tax rate on dividends.

CHAPTER 8

WORKING CAPITAL MANAGEMENT

SOLUTIONS

1. B is correct.

   Current ratio = Current assets/Current liabilities = Current assets/100 million = 2.5

   Therefore, current assets = €250 million.

   $$\text{Quick ratio} = (\text{Current assets} - \text{Inventory})/\text{Current liabilities}$$
   $$= (250 \text{ million} - \text{Inventory})/100 \text{ million} = 1.5$$

   Therefore, inventory = €100 million.

2. C is correct.
   Number of days of inventory = $2,300/($20,000/365) = 41.975 days
   Number of days of receivables = $2,500/($25,000/365) = 36.5 days
   Operating cycle = 41.975 + 36.5 days = 78.475 days
   Note: The net operating cycle is 47.9 days.
   Purchases = $20,000 + $2,300 − $2,000 = $20,300
   Number of days of payables = $1,700/($20,300/365) = 30.567 days
   The net operating cycle is 78.475 − 30.567 = 47.908 days.

3. A is correct.
   Number of days of inventory = $2,000/($30,000/365) = 24.333 days
   Number of days of receivables = $3,000/($40,000/365) = 27.375 days
   Operating cycle = 24.333 + 27.375 days = 51.708 days
   Purchases = $30,000 + $2,000 − $1,500 = $30,500
   Number of days of payables = $4,000/($30,500/365) = 47.869 days
   The net operating cycle is 51.708 − 47.869 = 3.839 days.

4. C is correct. Bond equivalent yield = [($10,000 − 9,725)/$9,725] × (365/182) = 5.671%.

5. C is correct. A higher level of uncollectible accounts may occur, but a longer average collection period will certainly occur.

6. C is correct.

$$\text{Cost} = \left(1 + \frac{0.02}{0.98}\right)^{365/40} - 1 = 20.24\%$$

7. B is correct.

$$\text{Line cost} = \frac{\text{Interest} + \text{Commitment fee}}{\text{Net proceeds}} \times 12$$

$$= \frac{(0.072 \times \$1,000,000 \times 1/12) + (0.005 \times \$1,000,000 \times 1/12)}{\$1,000,000} \times 12$$

$$= \frac{\$6,000 + 416.67}{\$1,000,000} \times 12 = 0.077 \text{ or } 7.7\%$$

$$\text{Banker's acceptance cost} = \frac{\text{Interest}}{\text{Net proceeds}} \times 12$$

$$= \frac{0.071 \times \$1,000,000 \times 1/12}{\$1,000,000 - (0.071 \times \$1,000,000 \times 1/12)} \times 12$$

$$= \frac{\$5,916.67}{\$994,083.33} \times 12 = 0.0714 \text{ or } 7.14\%$$

$$\text{Commercial paper cost} = \frac{\text{Interest} + \text{Dealer's commission} + \text{Back-up costs}}{\text{Net proceeds}} \times 12$$

$$= \frac{\begin{array}{c}(0.069 \times \$1,000,000 \times 1/12) + (0.0025 \times \$1,000,000 \times 1/12) \\ + (0.003333 \times \$1,000,000 \times 1/12)\end{array}}{\$1,000,000 - (0.069 \times \$1,000,000 \times 1/12)} \times 12$$

$$= \frac{\$5,750 + 208.33 + 277.78}{\$1,000,000 - 5,750} \times 12 = 0.0753 \text{ or } 7.53\%$$

8. B is correct.
   Company A: $1.0 million/($5.0 million/365) = 73.0 days
   Company B: $1.2 million/($3.0 million/365) = 146.0 days
   Company C: $0.8 million/($2.5 million/365) = 116.8 days
   Company D: $0.1 million/($0.5 million/365) = 73.0 days
9. B is correct.
   Company A: $6.0 million/$1.2 million = 5.00
   Company B: $4.0 million/$1.5 million = 2.67
   Company C: $3.0 million/$1.0 million = 3.00
   Company D: $0.6 million/$0.2 million = 3.00
10. B is correct.
    20X1: 73 days
    20X2: 70.393
    Note: If the number of days decreased from 20X1 to 20X2, the receivable turnover increased.

11. A is correct. Company B increased its accounts receivable (A/R) turnover and reduced its number of days of receivables between 20X1 and 20X2.

	20X1		20X2	
Company	A/R Turnover	Number of Days of Receivables	A/R Turnover	Number of Days of Receivables
A	5.000	73.000	5.000	73.000
B	2.500	146.000	2.667	136.875
C	3.125	116.800	3.000	121.667
D	5.000	73.000	3.000	121.667

12. B is correct.
   Company A number of days of inventory $= 100 - 73 = 27$ days.
   Company D number of days of inventory $= 145 - 121.67 = 23.33$ days.
   Company A's inventory turnover $= 365/27 = 13.5$ times.
   Company D's inventory turnover $= 365/23.3 = 15.6$ times.

CHAPTER 9

FINANCIAL STATEMENT ANALYSIS

SOLUTIONS

1. C is correct. To address this question, we need to first calculate the common-size percentages for the balance sheets in 2003 through 2005.

	2005	2004	2003
Cash, cash equiv., and marketable securities	0.6%	0.5%	0.4%
Accounts receivable	5.8%	4.7%	3.2%
Inventories	25.8%	25.9%	25.0%
Total current assets	32.3%	31.0%	28.6%
Net property, plant, and equipment	64.5%	65.5%	67.9%
Intangible assets	3.2%	3.4%	3.6%
Total assets	100.0%	100.0%	100.0%
Accounts payable	1.6%	2.7%	2.2%
Debt due in one year	3.2%	3.4%	3.6%
Long-term debt	38.7%	44.8%	50.0%
Shareholders' equity	56.5%	49.0%	42.6%
Total liabilities and equity	100.0%	100.0%	100.0%

Once we have these percentages, we can see the changing composition of the balance sheet over time:

Account	General Trend
Cash and equivalents	⇧
Accounts receivable	⇧
Inventories	⇧
Net property, plant, and equipment	⇩
Intangible assets	⇩
Accounts payable	⇩
Long-term debt	⇩
Shareholders' equity	⇧

2. B is correct.

	2005	2004	2003
Cost of sales as a percentage of sales	80.0%	81.8%	81.0%

3. B is correct.

	2005	2004	2003
Cost of sales as a percentage of 2003 cost of sales	117.6%	105.9%	100.0%

4. B is correct. The most significant benefit of using common-size statements is scaling, whether for a given company or over time. Common-size analysis allows us to make comparisons of investments, financing, and profitability between companies of different sizes and over time for a single company.

5. B is correct. We perform the calculations using the following relationship:

$$\frac{\text{Cost of goods sold}}{\text{Inventory}} \times \frac{\text{Inventory}}{\text{Cost of goods sold}/365} = 365$$

$$\text{Inventory turnover} \times \text{Number of days of inventory} = 365$$

Inserting the given information, we have

$$\text{Inventory turnover} \times 50 = 365$$

and solving for inventory turnover provides a turnover of 7.3 times.

6. B is correct. Compare the formulas for the operating cycle and the net operating cycle:

$$\text{Operating cycle} = \frac{\text{Number of days}}{\text{of inventory}} + \frac{\text{Number of days}}{\text{of receivables}}$$

$$\text{Net operating cycle} = \frac{\text{Number of days}}{\text{of inventory}} + \frac{\text{Number of days}}{\text{of receivables}} - \frac{\text{Number of days}}{\text{of payables}}$$

Therefore, the difference between the *operating cycle* and the *net operating cycle* is the number of days of payables.

7. C is correct.

$$\text{Net operating cycle} = \frac{\text{Number of days}}{\text{of inventory}} + \frac{\text{Number of days}}{\text{of receivables}} - \frac{\text{Number of days}}{\text{of payables}}$$

8. A is correct. Liquidity ratios measure the company's ability to meet its immediate financial demands, which are represented by current liabilities.

9. B is correct. Comparing the formulas of the two ratios, we see that they share the same denominator but have different numerators.

$$\text{Current ratio} = \frac{\text{Current assets}}{\text{Current liabilities}} \quad \text{vs.} \quad \text{Cash ratio} = \frac{\text{Cash and cash equivalents}}{\text{Current liabilities}}$$

The current ratio's numerator is equal to the cash and cash equivalents plus accounts receivable, inventories, and any other current assets. Therefore, the current ratio is greater than or equal to the cash ratio.

10. C is correct.

$$\text{Interest coverage ratio} = \frac{\text{Earnings before interest and taxes}}{\text{Interest payments}}$$

The given information provides earnings before taxes, so we must add interest to this amount to arrive at earnings before interest and taxes:

$$\text{Interest coverage ratio} = \frac{\$20 + \$2}{\$2} = \frac{\$22}{\$2} = 11 \text{ times}$$

11. C is correct. We are given information on the net profit margin:

$$\text{Net profit margin} = \frac{\text{Net income}}{\text{Revenues}} = 12\%$$

Using the net profit margin along with the tax rate, we can calculate the before-tax margin. Let t indicate the tax rate. Then:

$$\frac{\text{Net profit}}{\text{margin}} = \frac{\text{Net income}}{\text{Revenues}} = \frac{\text{Earnings before taxes } (1-t)}{\text{Revenues}} = \left(\frac{\text{Before-tax}}{\text{profit margin}}\right)(1-t)$$

$$\frac{\text{Before-tax}}{\text{profit margin}} = \frac{\text{Net profit margin}}{(1-t)}$$

Before-tax profit margin $= 0.12/(1 - 0.4) = 20.0\%$

12. B is correct.

$$\text{Operating return on assets} = \frac{\text{Operating income}}{\text{Total assets}} = \frac{\text{Revenues}}{\text{Total assets}} \times \frac{\text{Operating income}}{\text{Revenues}}$$

Operating return on assets $= 1.5 \times 4\% = 6.0\%$

13. C is correct. This is the DuPont triangle, in which profit margins and turnovers are used to explain returns.

14. A is correct.

$$\text{Return on equity} = \left(\frac{\text{Net income}}{\text{Revenues}} \times \frac{\text{Revenues}}{\text{Total assets}} \right) \times \frac{\text{Total assets}}{\text{Shareholders' equity}}$$

$$\text{Return on equity} = \text{Return on assets} \times \frac{\text{Total assets}}{\text{Shareholders' equity}}$$

15. A is correct.

$$\text{Return on equity} = \frac{\text{Net income}}{\text{Average total equity}} = \frac{\text{Net income}}{\text{Revenues}} \times \frac{\text{Revenues}}{\text{Average total assets}}$$

$$\times \frac{\text{Average total assets}}{\text{Average total equity}}$$

$$\text{Return on equity} = -5\% \times 1.5 \times 1.2 = -9.0\%$$

16. B is correct.

LaPearla Company Income Statement for Year 0 (in millions)

	2005	Percent of Sales	Pro Forma	Explanation
Revenues	€10,000	100.0	€11,000	110% of 2005 sales
Cost of goods sold	5,500	55.0	6,050	55% of projected sales
Gross profit	€4,500	45.0	€4,950	
Selling, general, and administrative expenses	800	8.0	880	8% of projected sales
Operating income	€3,700	37.0	€4,070	37% of projected sales
Interest expense	500	5.0	550	5% of projected sales
Earnings before taxes	€3,200		€3,520	
Taxes	960		1,056	30% of earnings before taxes
Net income	€2,240		€2,464	

Alternatively, rather than prepare an entire pro forma income statement, increase earnings before taxes by 10% because all elements of the income statement are sales driven. Then calculate the net income after taxes: €3,200(1.10)(0.7) = €2,464.

17. C is correct.

LaPearla Company Income Statement for Year 0 (in millions)

	2005	Percent of Sales	Pro forma	Explanation
Revenues	€10,000	100.0	€11,000	110% of 2005 sales
Cost of goods sold	5,500	55.0	6,050	55% of projected sales
Gross profit	€4,500	45.0	€4,950	
Selling, general, and administrative expenses	800	8.0	880	8% of projected sales
Operating income	€3,700	37.0	€4,070	37% of projected sales
Interest expense	500	5.0	500	Fixed because long-term debt is fixed
Earnings before taxes	€3,200		€3,570	
Taxes	960		1,071	30% of earnings before taxes
Net income	€2,240		€2,499	

Alternatively, €3,700(1.1) − €500(.07) = €2,499.

LaPearla Company Balance Sheet, End of Year 0 (in millions)

	2005	Percent of Sales	Pro Forma	Explanation
Current assets	€2,000	20.0	€2,200	20% of projected sales
Net plant and equipment	18,000	180.0	19,800	180% of projected sales
Total assets	€20,000	200.0	€22,000	200% of projected sales
Current liabilities	€1,000	10.0	€1,100	10% of projected sales
Long-term debt	5,000		5,000	Fixed at €5,000
Common stock and paid-in capital	500		500	Fixed at €500
Retained earnings	13,500			
Total liabilities and equity	€20,000	200.0	€22,000	200% of projected sales

No dividends: Financing surplus
Without paying dividends,

$$\text{Retained earnings} = €13,500 + €2,499 = €15,999$$

With no dividends:

Total liabilities and equity	€22,000
Less:	
Current liabilities	1,100
Long-term debt	5,000
Common stock and paid-in capital	500
Retained earnings without dividends	15,999
Financing deficiency or (surplus)	(€599)

Paying 50% of net income in dividends: Financing deficiency
Paying 50% of net income as dividends,

$$\text{Retained earnings} = €13,500 + €2,499 - €1,249.5 = €14,749.5$$

Total liabilities and equity	€22,000.0
Less:	
Current liabilities	1,100.0
Long-term debt	5,000.0
Common stock and paid-in capital	500.0
Retained earnings with dividends	14,749.5
Financing deficiency or (surplus)	€650.5

Paying 100% of net income as dividends: Financing deficiency
Paying 100% of net income as dividends,

Total liabilities and equity	€22,000
Less:	
Current liabilities	1,100
Long-term debt	5,000
Common stock and paid-in capital	500
Retained earnings with dividends	13,500
Financing deficiency or (surplus)	€1,900

CHAPTER 10

MERGERS AND ACQUISITIONS

SOLUTIONS

1. C is correct. These are conglomerate and horizontal mergers, respectively.

2. C is correct. EPS is $2.63. Because Modern Auto's stock price is $40 and Sky Systems' stock price is $25, Modern Auto will acquire Sky Systems by exchanging 1 of its shares for $40/25 = 1.60$ shares of Sky Systems. There are 15 million shares of Sky Systems. Their acquisition will take $15/1.60 = 9.375$ million shares of Modern Auto. The total number of shares after the merger $= 49.375$ million. The EPS after the merger $= 130/49.375 = \$2.63$.

3. A is correct. Both of the statements by Wilhelm are wrong. The first statement is wrong because diversification by itself does not lower risk for shareholders. Investors can diversify very cheaply on their own by purchasing stocks of different companies (for example, a Modern Auto shareholder could purchase stocks of Sky Systems).

   The second statement is also wrong. The P/E ratio will not necessarily remain the same following the merger and is more likely to decline. The premerger P/E for Modern Auto is $40/2.50 = 16$. After the merger, the EPS would be $130 million/49.375 million shares, or 2.6329. The post-merger P/E will probably fall to $40/2.6329 = 15.19$.

4. C is correct. HiFly is a white knight.

5. A is correct.

   Target shareholders' gain = Premium = $P_T - V_T$

   P_T = Price paid for the target company = $400 million as provided in the vignette

   V_T = Pre-merger value of the target = $25 share price $\times$ 15 million shares
       = $375 million

   $400 million $-$ $375 million = $25 million

6. C is correct. The pre- and post-merger HHI measures are 1,550 and 1,950, respectively. Not only is the HHI increasing by 400 points, but the industry concentration level also moves from moderately to highly concentrated. The probable action by the regulatory authorities is thus a challenge.

	Pre-Merger			Post-Merger	
Company	Market Share	Market Share Squared	Company	Market Share	Market Share Squared
1	25%	625	1	25%	625
2 (HiFly)	20%	400	2 & 3 (combined)	30%	900
3 (Sky)	10%	100	4	10%	100
4	10%	100	5	10%	100
5	10%	100	6	10%	100
6	10%	100	7	10%	100
7	10%	100	8	5%	25
8	5%	25			
	HHI =	**1,550**		**HHI =**	**1,950**

7. C is correct. The estimated stock value is $41.57. The value of High Tech = Total PV (present value) of free cash flows during the first four years + PV of the terminal value of High Tech at the end of the fourth year using the constant growth model.

Total PV of free cash flows during the first four years = $15/1.11 + 17/1.11^2 + 20/1.11^3 + 23/1.11^4 = \$57.09$ million.

Based on the constant growth model, the terminal value (TV) of High Tech at the end of the fourth year is $TV = FCF$ at the end of the fifth year$/(k - g) = (23 \times 1.065)/(0.11 - 0.065) = \$544.33$ million.

PV of the terminal value $= 544.33/1.11^4 = \$358.57$ million.

Estimated value of High Tech $= 57.09 + 358.57 = \$415.66$ million.

Estimated stock price $= 415.66$ million/10 million shares $= \$41.57$.

8. B is correct. The estimated stock price is $40.56.

Total PV of free cash flows during the first four years = $15/1.11 + 17/1.11^2 + 20/1.11^3 + 23/1.11^4 = \$57.09$ million.

Based on the cash flow multiple method, the terminal value of High Tech four years later $= 23 \times 23 = \$529$ million.

PV of the terminal value $= 529/1.11^4 = \$348.47$ million.

Estimated value of High Tech = Total PV of free cash flows during the first four years + PV of the terminal value at the end of the fourth year $= 57.09 + 348.47 = \$405.55$ million.

Estimated stock price $= 405.55$ million/10 million shares $= \$40.56$.

9. A is correct. The estimated value is $35.21. First, calculate the relative valuation ratios for the three comparable companies and their means.

Relative Valuation Ratio	Alpha	Neutron	Techno	Mean
P/E	14.62	13.69	20.24	16.18
P/S	2.18	1.62	2.81	2.20
P/BV	2.90	3.20	4.57	3.56

Then apply the means to the valuation variables for High Tech to get the estimated stock price for High Tech based on the comparable companies.

Valuation Variables	High Tech	Mean Multiple for Comparables	Estimated Stock Price
Current stock price	31.00		
Earnings/share	1.98	16.18	32.04
Sales/share	17.23	2.20	37.91
Book value/share	10.02	3.56	35.67

The mean estimated stock price is $(32.04 + 37.91 + 35.67)/3 = \$35.21$.

10. C is correct. The price is $41.29. The takeover premiums on three recent comparable takeovers are:

$$(28.00 - 24.90)/24.90 = 12.45\%$$

$$(52.00 - 43.20)/43.20 = 20.37\%$$

$$(34.50 - 29.00)/29.00 = 18.97\%$$

$$\text{Mean takeover premium} = 17.26\%$$

Using the comparable company approach, the stock price of High Tech if it is traded at the mean of the comparable company valuations is $35.21. Considering the mean takeover premium, the estimated fair acquisition price for High Tech is $35.21 \times 1.1726 = \$41.29$.

11. B is correct. The fair acquisition price is $40.86. First, calculate the relative valuation ratios based on the acquisition price for the three comparable transactions and their means.

Relative Valuation Ratio	Quadrant	ProTech	Automator	Mean
P/E	20.00	24.76	14.68	19.81
P/S	2.65	2.55	2.17	2.46
P/BV	3.38	5.13	3.76	4.09

Then apply the means to the valuation variables for High Tech to get the estimated acquisition price for High Tech based on the comparable transactions.

Valuation Variables	High Tech	Mean Multiple Paid for Comparables	Estimated Acquisition Price
Earnings/share	1.98	19.81	39.22
Sales/share	17.23	2.46	42.39
Book value/share	10.02	4.09	40.98

The mean estimated acquisition stock price is $(39.22 + 42.39 + 40.98)/3 = \$40.86$.

12. A is correct. Both of Smith's statements are incorrect. If there was a pre-announcement run-up in Quadrant's price because of speculation, the takeover premium should be computed based on the price prior to the run-up. Because the comparable transaction approach is based on the acquisition price, the takeover premium is implicitly recognized in this approach.

13. B is correct. Value is $39.30.

$$\text{Average P/E ratio is } 21.33 = (23.00 + 19.50 + 21.50)/3$$

$$\text{Value based on P/E ratio} = 21.33\,(1.75) = 37.33$$

$$\text{Average P/B ratio is } 4.80 = (4.24 + 5.25 + 4.91)/3$$

$$\text{Value based on P/B ratio} = 4.80\,(8.50) = 40.80$$

$$\text{Average P/CF ratio is } 12.43 = (12.60 + 11.40 + 13.30)/3$$

$$\text{Value based on P/CF ratio} = 12.43\,(3.20) = 39.79$$

Because Zin believes each valuation ratio is equally valid, value is a simple average of the three values.

$$\text{Value} = (37.33 + 40.80 + 39.79)/3 = 39.30$$

14. C is correct. An equity carve-out involves sale of equity in a new legal entity to outsiders, and would thus result in a cash inflow for Moonbase. A spin-off or a split-off does not generate a cash flow to the firm.

15. B is correct. The first comment about the poison pill is correct, but the second comment is incorrect. Shareholders do not "put" their shares to the company; rather, bondholders can exercise the put in the event of a hostile takeover. Bondholders have the right to sell their bonds back to the target at a redemption price that is prespecified in the bond indenture, typically at or above par value.

16. C is correct. Statement #3 provides the most support for a strong governance rating. The statement describes the manner in which the audit committee should work. The other two statements do not support a strong governance rating, as each casts doubt about the independence of the board from management's control.

17. B is correct. The second policy is least likely to ensure effective contributions from the board. The board through self-assessment, and not management, should assess the board's performance.

18. A is correct. As an independent director, without an interlocking relationship and with the expertise required, Steris would be eligible to serve on either of the two committees.

19. A is correct.

$$\text{PV of first three cash flows}: 5/1.15 + 6/1.15^2 + 7/1.15^3 = 13.49$$

$$\text{Terminal value}: 7 \times 10 = 70$$

$$\text{PV of terminal value}:= 70/1.15^3 = 46.03$$

$$\text{Value} = 13.49 + 46.03 = 59.52$$

$$\text{Value per share} = 59.52/1.2 = 49.60$$

20. B is correct.

> Terminal value at 5 percent: $7(1.05)/(0.15 - 0.05) = 73.50\text{M}$
>
> Terminal value at 0 percent: $7/0.15 = 46.67\text{M}$
>
> Change in present value: $(46.67 - 73.50)/1.15^3 = -17.64$
>
> Percentage change: $-17.64/61.8 = -28.5\%$

21. B is correct.

Step 1. Compute valuation ratios:

Valuation Ratio	Alphatech	Betatech	Mean
P/E	36.00	30.00	33.00
P/S	2.25	2.00	2.125
P/BV	4.00	4.50	4.25

Step 2. Apply to Durtech's variables:

Valuation Ratio	Durtech	Mean Multiple	Estimated Stock Price
Earnings per share	1.00	33.00	33.00
Sales per share	16.00	2.125	34.00
Book value per share	8.00	4.25	34.00

Step 3. Determine mean value: $(33 + 34 + 34)/3 = \$33.67$ per share

22. B is correct. A comparable transaction sells for a premium of $55/44.4 - 1 = 23.9\%$.
23. C is correct. Omegatech's transaction P/E ratio: $55/1.25 = 44$. So estimated fair acquisition value per share is $44 \times 1 = \$44.00$.
24. B is correct. Possible government action is based on the change in the HHI and the post-merger HHI.

ABOUT THE
CFA PROGRAM

The Chartered Financial Analyst® designation (CFA®) is a globally recognized standard of excellence for measuring the competence and integrity of investment professionals. To earn the CFA charter, candidates must successfully pass through the CFA Program, a global graduate-level self-study program that combines a broad curriculum with professional conduct requirements as preparation for a wide range of investment specialties.

Anchored by a practice-based curriculum, the CFA Program is focused on the knowledge identified by professionals as essential to the investment decision-making process. This body of knowledge maintains current relevance through a regular, extensive survey of practicing CFA charterholders across the globe. The curriculum covers 10 general topic areas, ranging from equity and fixed-income analysis to portfolio management to corporate finance, all with a heavy emphasis on the application of ethics in professional practice. Known for its rigor and breadth, the CFA Program curriculum highlights principles common to every market so that professionals who earn the CFA designation have a thoroughly global investment perspective and a profound understanding of the global marketplace.

www.cfainstitute.org

CFA Institute
+ Wiley
= Success

John Wiley & Sons and CFA Institute are proud to present the **CFA Institute Investment Series** geared specifically for industry professionals and graduate-level students. This cutting-edge series focuses on the most important topics in the finance industry. The authors of these books are themselves leading industry professionals and academics who bring their wealth of knowledge and expertise to you.

The series provides clear, practitioner-driven coverage of the knowledge and skills critical to investment analysts, portfolio managers, and financial advisors.

978-1-118-10537-5
Hardcover
$95.00 US
$114.00 CAN
£65.00 UK

978-1-118-11197-0
Paper
$45.00 US
$54.00 CAN
£30.99 UK

978-0-470-91580-6
$95.00 US
$114.00 CAN/£65.00 UK

978-0-470-62400-5
$95.00 US
$114.00 CAN/£65.00 UK

978-0-470-57143-9
$95.00 US
$114.00 CAN/£65.00 UK

978-0-470-05220-4
$95.00 US
$104.00 CAN/£65.00 UK

978-0-470-05221-1
$95.00 US
$104.99 CAN/£65.00 UK

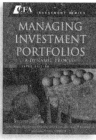

978-0-470-08014-6
$100.00 US
$119.99 CAN/£70.00 UK

978-0-470-91662-9
$95.00 US
$114.00 CAN/£65.00 UK

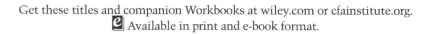

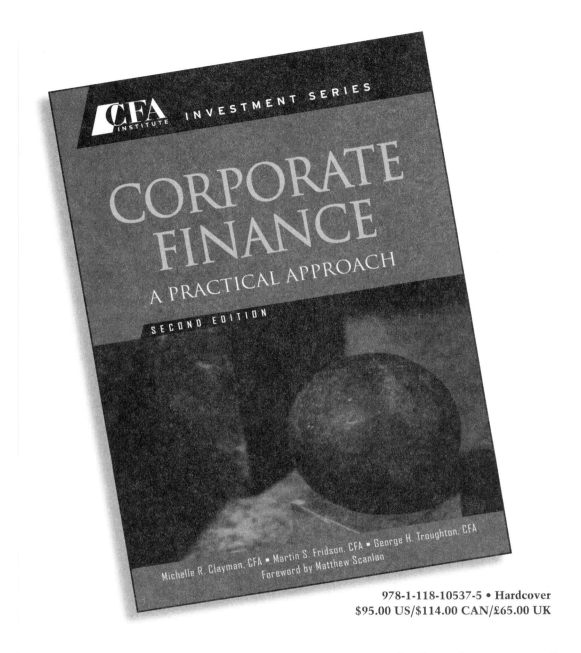